Adventures in Phonics
Second Edition

Level
B

Florence Lindstrom

TEACHER'S MANUAL

A publication of

Christian Liberty Press

502 West Euclid Avenue
Arlington Heights, Illinois 60004
www.christianlibertypress.com
www.shopchristianliberty.com

Written by Florence M. Lindstrom
Editing and layout by Edward J. Shewan
Copyediting by Diane C. Olson
Cover design by Bob Fine
Cover image © Design Pics 2013,

ISBN 978-1-935796-34-3

Printed in the United States of America

Introduction

Page 1

The primary goal of phonics instruction is to help the student become a strong reader by teaching him the *sounds* made by individual letters and the combinations of letters. This will enable him to sound out an unlimited number of words. Emphasis should be placed upon teaching the *sound* of each letter and not its name. Only the *sounds* of the letters help us read words. Once your student understands the basic rules of phonics, the world of reading will open up to him. This will also enable him to be a good speller.

It is important for teachers to follow the instructions located in this **Teacher's Manual** as a preparation for the daily lessons in *Adventures in Phonics Level B*. Keep in mind that students learn at varying rates of speed depending on their previous schooling, their maturity, and the difficulty of the lesson. If your student has completed *Adventures in Phonics Level A*, then the first 129 pages will serve as a review and reinforcement of that workbook. If this, however, is the first exposure to learning the sounds of the letters and to reading, the student may need extra drill and review. In this case, the student should use the flashcards, which can be removed from the back of this **Teacher's Manual**. Spend as much time as you feel necessary to help your student understand each lesson.

In the student's workbook, the pages have been perforated so that they can easily be removed to help the student in completing his work. All the student's work should be carefully saved for review purposes.

The two most important attributes of a phonics teacher are loving patience and caring perseverance. May the Lord grant you, the instructor, an abundant supply of both.

Florence Lindstrom
Arlington Heights, Illinois

Purpose

Teach the recognition, sound, and formation of the short vowel **a**.

Before class begins

1. Remove flashcard **A a** from the set of flashcards.

2. Open to the first page.

Lesson

Enthusiastically explain that the **A a** is one of the five vowels that are so important in reading. Vowels have several sounds, but the short sounds will be learned first. Ask the student to repeat the sound three times after you as you point at the three ways it is printed (**A**, **a**, and **a**). This sound is heard at the beginning of **a**-pple, **a**-nt, **a**-nswer. In the shaded box near the upper left-hand side of the page, the top letter shows how people print the capital or *upper-case* letter **A**—used at the beginning of a person's name such as **A**ndrew or **A**nna. The bottom letter shows how people print the *lower-case* letter **a**.

Place the flashcard near the work area so it is seen as the page is being studied.

Follow the directions and complete the work.

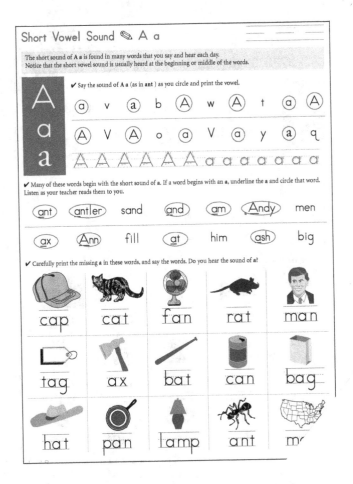

Page 2

Purpose

Teach the recognition, sound, and formation of the short vowel **e**.

Before class begins

1. Remove flashcard **E e** from the set at the back of this manual.
2. Open to page 2.

Lesson

Review the **A a** flashcard with your student, saying it five times. Say the short sound of **E e** as you introduce that flashcard, having the student repeat it after you. Drill with both cards, listening to hear that the student can distinguish between the two sounds.

Have him repeat after you: **e**-gg, **e**-nd, **E**-mily, **e**-mpty, **e**-lephant, **e**-lbow, etc., taking additional examples from the worksheet if needed.

Follow the directions and complete the work.

Page 3

Purpose

Teach the recognition, sound, and formation of the short vowel **i**.

Before class begins

1. Remove flashcard **I i** from the set at the back of this manual.
2. Open to page 3.

Lesson

Review the **A a** and **E e** flashcards with your student, saying them five times. Say the short sound of **I i** as you introduce that flashcard, having the student repeat it after you. Drill with all three cards, listening to hear that the student can distinguish between the three sounds.

Have him repeat after you: **i**-nch, **i**-nvite, **i**-n, **i**-tch, **i**-nside, **i**-nner, etc., taking additional examples from the worksheet if needed.

Follow the directions as you have the student complete the lesson.

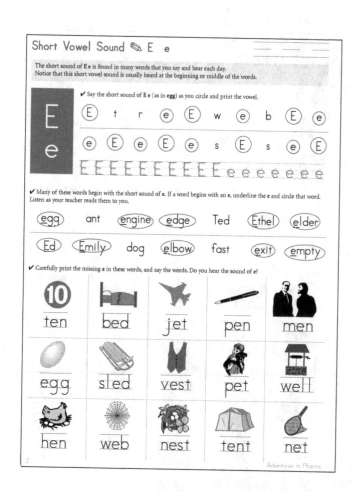

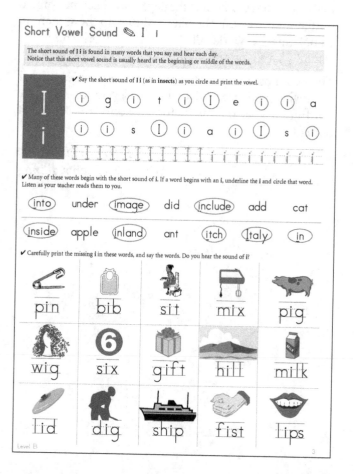

Page 4

Purpose

Teach the recognition, sound, and formation of the short vowel **o**.

Before class begins

1. Remove flashcard **O o** from the set at the back of this manual.

2. Open to page 4.

Lesson

Review the flashcards for **A a**, **E e**, and **I i**, listening closely to hear that the sounds are said correctly. Introduce the **O o** flashcard, saying the short sound of **O o**, which is heard at the beginning of **O**-ctober, **o**-n, **o**-bject, **O**-scar, and **o**-ctopus. Before the student begins to print the vowel **o**, explain that he should begin by thinking about the 2 on a clock and proceeding backward to the 2 again.

Follow the directions and complete the lesson.

Page 5

Purpose

Review the first four vowels and teach the recognition, sound, and formation of the short vowel **u**.

Before class begins

1. Remove flashcard **U u** from the set at the back of this manual.

2. Open to page 5.

Lesson

Review the **A a**, **E e**, **I i**, and **O o** flashcards. Introduce the **U u** shape and sound. You may want to test the student by having him point to the correct flashcard as you say words like the following: **A**-frica, **u**-s, **i**-nch, **E**-sther, **A**-dam, **o**-live, **e**-dge, **u**-nder, **a**-fter, **o**-nward, **I**-ndian, **u**-ncle, etc.

Follow the directions as you have the student complete the lesson.

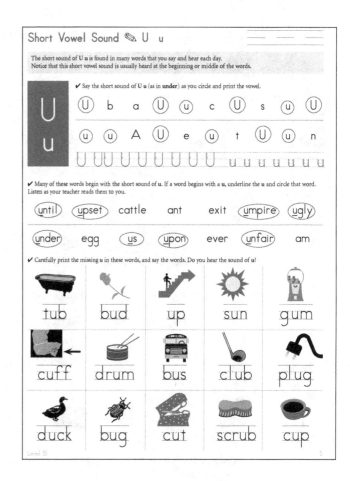

Page 6

Purpose

Teach the recognition, sound, and formation of the consonant **s**.

Before class begins

Open to page 6 and have the flashcard **S s** ready to add to the short vowel flashcards.

Lesson

Briefly discuss that the letters belong in two different groups: **vowels** and **consonants**. The first consonant that will be learned is the **S s**. Some important words that begin with this consonant are: **S**aviour, **S**pirit, **s**alvation, **s**in, **s**criptures, **s**oul, and **s**ermon.

Read the following sentences to your student:

> **S**even **s**andy **s**ea gulls **s**at **s**till on a **s**ilver **s**ailboat.

> **S**ee the **s**ix **s**nails **s**leep **s**ilently on the **s**oft **s**and at the **s**unny **s**easide.

Follow the directions and complete the top half of the page. Practice doing the bottom section orally so that the student will learn the beginning consonant/vowel sound before he completes that section by himself.

After completing the lesson, spend additional drill time by "reading" **sa**, **se**, **si**, **so**, and **su**.

Page 7

Purpose

Teach the recognition, sound, and formation of the consonant **t**.

Before class begins

Open to page 7 and have the flashcard **T t** ready.

Lesson

Begin the lesson by asking these questions: "How many toes do you have?" "What do we like to do on the telephone?" "What would be fun to sleep in out in the backyard?" "What needs to be on our suitcase to show that it belongs to us?" Show the **T t** flashcard and print it on the board, telling that letters are usually formed from the top.

Have the student repeat each of the following words and the sentence as you say them:

> **T**estament, **t**ower, **t**iger, **t**ennis, **T**exas, **t**each, **t**abernacle, **t**urkey, **t**ooth, **T**ommy, **T**eresa, **T**uesday

> **T**en **t**imid **t**urtles **t**raveled **t**oward a **t**all **t**unnel on **T**uesday.

Follow the directions and complete the top half of the page. Practice doing the bottom section orally, so the student will learn the beginning consonant or vowel sound before he completes that section by himself.

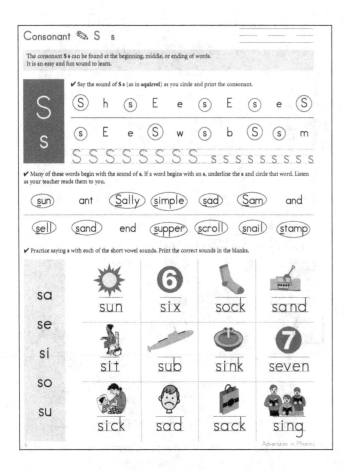

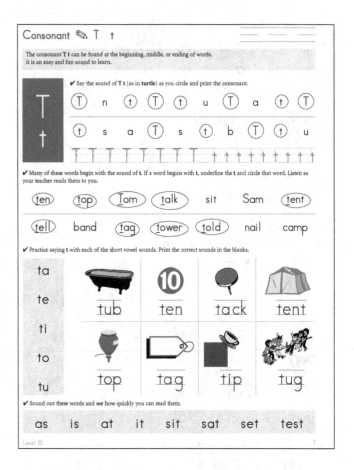

Page 8

Purpose

Teach the recognition, sound, and formation of the consonant **b**.

Before class begins

Open to page 8 and have the flashcard **B b** ready to add to the short vowel flashcards.

Lesson

Ask the student, "What is the most important book that God wants us to read?" (Bible) "Yes, the **B**ible is the **b**est **b**ook." Show him the **B b** flashcard and tell him that this is the consonant that says that beginning sound. Add this flashcard to the drill stack and have him practice saying them. Have your student repeat after you, as you say these wonderful things that God has given to us for a **b**lessing: **b**anana, **b**erries, **b**utter, **b**eans, **b**ears, **b**eagle, and **b**est of all—**b**abies.

Help the student print these words:

bat   bit   but   sat   set   sit

Follow the directions and complete the top half of the page. Practice doing the bottom section orally, so the student will learn the beginning consonant/vowel sound before he completes that section by himself.

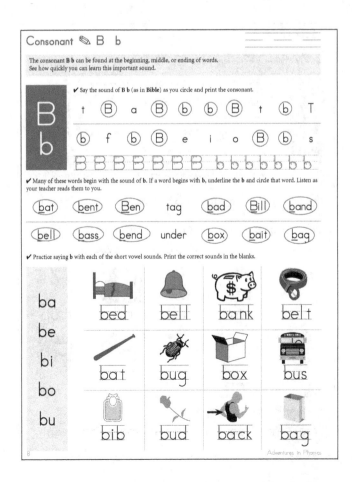

Page 9

Purpose

Teach the recognition, sound, and formation of the consonant **h**.

Before class begins

Open to page 9 and have the flashcard **H h** ready to add to the "known" flashcards.

Lesson

Ask the student, "Where will we live forever with Jesus if we love Him?" (**H**eaven). Tell him that each time we say this letter we let breath out of our mouth. Show him the **H h** flashcard and how to print the letter. Have him repeat after you as you say:

Happy Herman has hundreds of healthy hens in his hen house.

Herbert helped Harvey haul a heavy helicopter to the hangar.

Help your student to print these words on the board or paper.

hat   hit   hot   hut   hen
hub   tub   bus   sub   sit

Complete the page, working the bottom section orally before using a pencil.

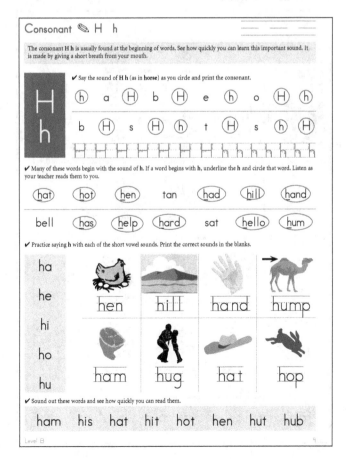

Page 10

Purpose

Teach the recognition, sound, and formation of the consonant **f**.

Before class begins

Open to page 10 and have the flashcard **F f** ready to add to the "known" flashcards.

Lesson

Say: "Listen to the funny sound that comes out between our top teeth and bottom lip as this new sound is made. **F**red and his **f**ather proudly **f**lew their **f**lag from the **f**ront porch for the **F**ourth of July. To have **f**riends, one must be **f**riendly."

Ask the student to listen for this sound at the end or in the middle of these words: lea**f**, cal**f**, stu**ff**, loa**f**, roo**f**, co**ff**ee, mu**ff**in, pu**ff**ing.

Teach the formation of this consonant, beginning from the top of the letter. Help the student to print the following words on a board or paper. If it is too difficult, print them slowly yourself to show how the words look. Be generous with encouragement and gentle with corrections.

fat   fit   fast

Complete the page, working the bottom section orally before using a pencil.

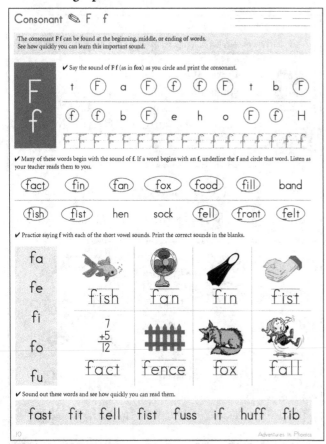

Page 11

Purpose

Teach the recognition, sound, and formation of the consonant **m**.

Before class begins

Open to page 11 and have the flashcard **M m** ready to add to the "known" flashcards.

Lesson

As you hold the **M m** flashcard, show with your lips how this consonant is formed by saying:

> **M**ary's **m**other **m**ade **m**eatballs on **M**onday.

> **M**olly **m**ade a **m**ess and **m**ust **m**op.

> **M**any **m**usicians played **m**arvelous **m**usic at the **m**arriage of **M**ichael and **M**artha.

Quickly drill all the flashcards. Help the student to print the following words as you slowly say them.

mat	am	mom	ham	hem
met	him	hum	must	mum

Complete the page, working the bottom section orally before using a pencil.

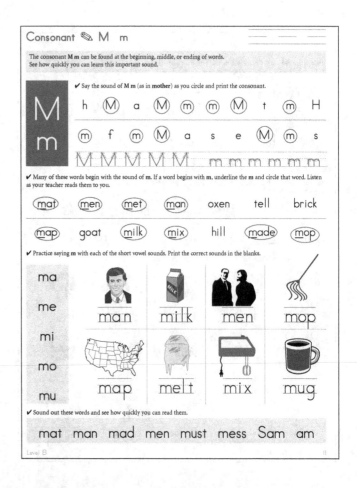

Page 12

Purpose

Teach the recognition, sound, and formation of the consonants **c** and **k**.

Before class begins

Open to page 12 and have the flashcards **C c** and **K k** ready to learn.

Lesson

As you show these cards, say that both of these consonants can make the same sound. Read this sentence. Point at the words to show your student as you read this sentence.

> God **c**reated all the **c**reatures such as the **c**rocodile, **c**row, **k**iwi, **c**ougar, **c**ricket, **c**ondor, **c**ockatoo, **k**angaroo, **k**udu, **k**oala, **c**amel, **c**ow, **k**atydid, and **c**aterpillar.

The **k** usually makes the **k** sound if it is followed by **e** or **i** as in **k**ey and **k**ing.

The **c** usually makes the **k** sound if it is followed by **a**, **o**, or **u** as in **c**at, **c**ot, and **c**ut.

Complete the page, working the bottom section orally before using a pencil.

Page 13

Purpose

Teach the recognition, sound, and formation of the consonants **c** and **k**.

Before class begins

Open to page 13 and have the flashcards **C c** and **K k** ready to learn.

Lesson

As you show these cards, say that both of these consonants can make the same sound. Read this sentence. Point at the words to show your student as you read this sentence.

> God **c**reated all the **c**reatures such as the **c**rocodile, **c**row, **k**iwi, **c**ougar, **c**ricket, **c**ondor, **c**ockatoo, **k**angaroo, **k**udu, **k**oala, **c**amel, **c**ow, **k**atydid, and **c**aterpillar.

The **k** usually makes the **k** sound if it is followed by **e** or **i** as in **k**ey and **k**ing.

The **c** usually makes the **k** sound if it is followed by **a**, **o**, or **u** as in **c**at, **c**ot, and **c**ut.

Complete the page, working the bottom section orally before using a pencil.

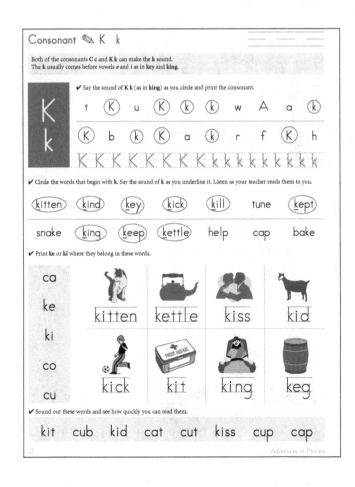

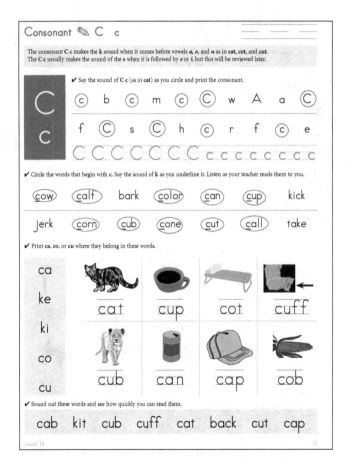

Page 14

Purpose

Teach the recognition, sound, and formation of the consonant **d**.

Before class begins

Open to page 14 and have the flashcard **D d** ready.

Lesson

Quickly drill all the consonant flashcards, especially noting the **b** flashcard. Show the **d** flashcard as you read these sentences:

> **D**aniel **d**id not **d**isobey and was **d**elivered by God from being **d**estroyed by lions in the **d**en.

> **D**avid's **d**og **d**igs **d**eep holes in the **d**irt.

Spend time helping the student to learn the difference between **d** and **b**.

Slowly dictate these words or print them yourself for the student to read.

dot	dim	did	sad	bad
mad	dad	had	dab	sob

Complete the page, working the bottom section orally before using a pencil.

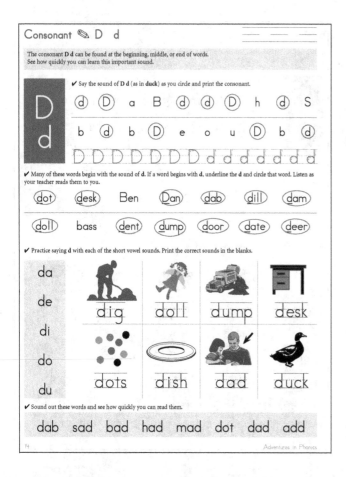

Page 15

Purpose

Teach the recognition, sound, and formation of the consonant **j**.

Before class begins

Open to page 15 and have the flashcard **J j** ready.

Lesson

As you show the **J j** flashcard say: "Our new sound is heard at the beginning of **J**esus." Ask the student to repeat after you some of the other names that come from the Bible:

> Jehovah, Joseph, Joshua, Jonah, James, Jacob, Jesse, John, Jeremiah, Judah, Joel, Jedediah, Jael, Jezebel, Jehoshaphat, and Job.

Also read:

> January, June, and July are months.

> Jeremiah likes to eat Jell-o®, jam, and jelly.

> Julie joyfully joined Janet to jump rope.

Slowly dictate these words or print them yourself for the student to read.

jet	jam	job	just	jab	jell

Complete the page, working the bottom section orally before using a pencil.

Page 16

Purpose

Teach the recognition, sound, and formation of the consonant **r**.

Before class begins

Open to page 16 and have the flashcard **R r** ready.

Lesson

As you show the **R r** flashcard, have the student repeat after you:

> Ruth was a reaper.
>
> Ralph's red roses are rare.
>
> Robert's rubber raft rocked and made a ripple on the river.
>
> Richard saw a rainbow above his roof.
>
> Rosa's ruby ring rolled right under a round rock.

Teach how the letters **R r** should be printed. Can your student print these words?

> ran   red   rug   rock   rat   rim

Complete the page, working the bottom section orally before using a pencil.

Page 17

Purpose

Teach the recognition, sound, and formation of the consonant **g**.

Before class begins

Open to page 17 and have the flashcard **G g** ready.

Lesson

As you show the **G g** flashcard, say: "Our **g**reat and **g**racious **G**od made every **g**ood thing."

Ask the students to repeat after you:

> Grace gave gold gifts to the good girls.
>
> Gray geese got goodies from the garden.
>
> Grant's goat gobbled green grapes and grass.

After you teach how to print **G g**, help the student to print these words:

> God   gift   get   gas   got
> hug   tag   big   beg   tug

Complete the page, working the bottom section orally before using a pencil.

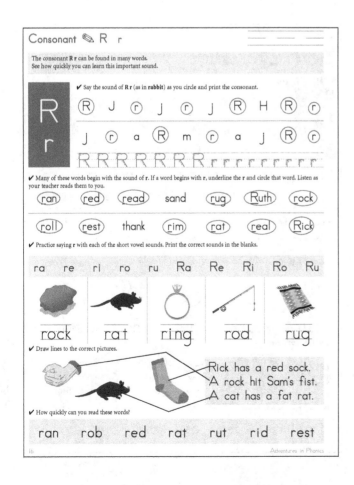

Page 18

Purpose

Teach the recognition, sound, and formation of the consonant **l**.

Before class begins

Open to page 18 and have the flashcard **L l** ready.

Lesson

As you introduce this sound, ask the student to repeat these sentences after you:

> The Lord is my light.
>
> I love the law of my Lord.
>
> The Bible is a lamp and a light for my life.

Also say:

> Lois likes licorice and lemon lollipops.
>
> Larry laughed loudly as his lambs leaped lightly over leaves on the lawn.

An important lesson to teach is that the letter **l** is *doubled* when it is at the end of short vowel words. Write these words for reading:

hill	mill	fill	doll	dull
sell	tell	fell	bell	gull

Complete the page, working the bottom section orally before using a pencil.

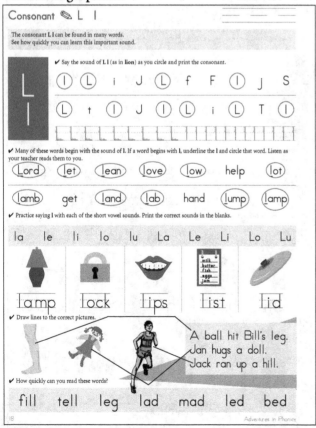

Page 19

Purpose

Teach the recognition, sound, and formation of the consonant **n**.

Before class begins

Open to page 19 and have the flashcard **N n** ready.

Lesson

Say this sound several times as you teach how to print it.

Ask your student, "What rhyming words beginning with the letter **n** answer the following sentences?"

A cat on my lap Took a long (**nap**).	Ned bought a pickle For just one (**nickel**).
The white purse Belongs to a (**nurse**).	Nancy smelled a rose With her (**nose**).

Help the student spell these words on a paper or board:

nut	net	not	nap	ten	tan

Complete the page, working the bottom section orally before using a pencil.

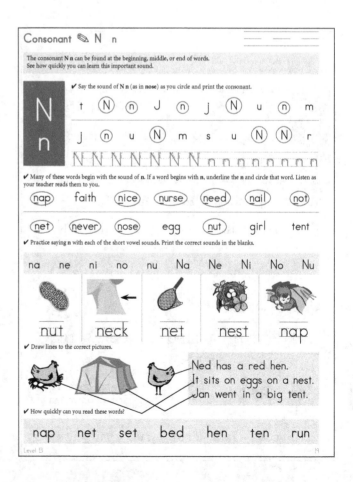

Page 20

Purpose

Teach the recognition, sound, and formation of the consonant **w**.

Before class begins

Open to page 20 and have the flashcard **W w** ready.

Lesson

Show the **W w** flashcard and say that this letter is fun to draw—going down, up, down, up. Have your student repeat the following sentences after you:

> God made our wonderful world.

> Wendy and William watched a woman wash wide windows with water from the well on Wednesday in West Wellington.

Ask him to listen and say after you these places that begin with the consonant **w**:

> Wyoming, Winnipeg, Williamsburg, Wittenberg, Wales, and Winston.

After the student practices printing **W w**, help him to print these words:

wet	well	will	wag	went
web	wed	wig	win	west

Complete the page, working the bottom section orally before using a pencil.

---

* Note that *win* or *won* may be used under the **runner** in the middle of page 20, even though this sound of **o** has not been taught yet.

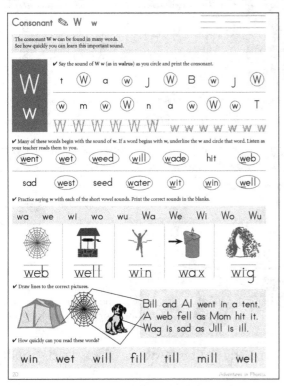

Page 21

Purpose

Teach the recognition, sound, and formation of the consonant **p**.

Before class begins

Open to page 21 and have the flashcard **P p** ready.

Lesson

As you show this flashcard say, "Our li**p**s come together as we begin to make this sound. We **p**raise God in our **p**rayers for His **p**erfect **p**lans."

Have the student listen closely as you say:

> Peter and Paul packed plenty of food for a picnic in the park in Portland. They brought pop, pickles, potato chips, peanuts, Popsicles®, pears, pizza, pretzels, peaches, pumpkin pie, and popcorn.

Teach the student how to print **P p** and help him to print these words on a paper or board.

pan	pet	pig	pad	pill
map	mop	cup	top	dip

Complete the page, working the bottom section orally before using a pencil.

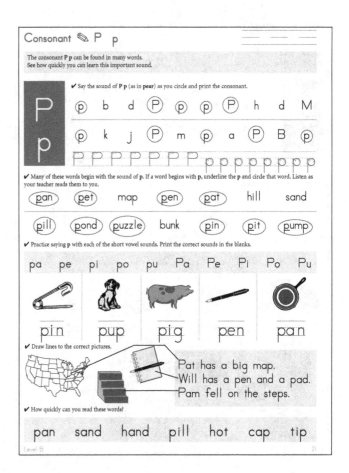

Page 22

Purpose

Teach the recognition, sound, and formation of the consonant **v**.

Before class begins

Open to page 22 and have the flashcard **V v** ready.

Lesson

As you show the **V v** flashcard and say its sound, have the student listen and slowly repeat:

> Victoria and Virginia visited Valerie's vineyard and vegetable garden in a vacant lot in the village down in a valley.

> Verna put violets and vines in a very nice vase and vacuumed the veranda.

> Victor put his violin into his van.

Help the student to print these words:

> van   vest   vet   vast   vent

Complete the page, working the bottom section orally before using a pencil.

Page 23

Purpose

Teach the recognition, sound, and formation of the consonant **q**.

Before class begins

Open to page 23 and have the flashcard **Qu qu** ready.

Lesson

As you show this flashcard, teach that in English the consonant **q** is almost always followed by the vowel **u**.* Have the student repeat after you as you say these words:

> quest   quart   quail
> quick   quill   quit

Complete the page, working the bottom section orally before using a pencil.

---

* Explain that there are a number of words in English with the consonant *q* that are not followed by the vowel *u*. For example, the word *qwerty* is the name for the layout of a standard English keyboard. This word comes from the first six letters on the top row of letters on the keyboard. Besides, several foreign words from Arabic, Hebrew, and other languages have come into English that do not follow this rule: burqa, qabab, etc.

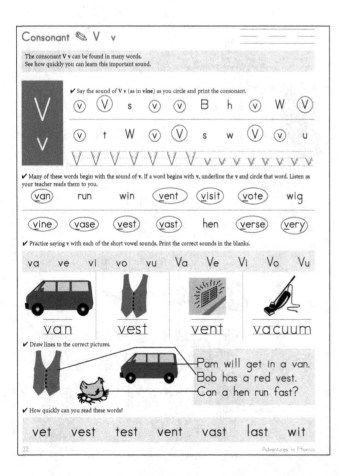

Page 24

Purpose

Teach the recognition, sound, and formation of the consonant **y**.

Before class begins

Open to page 24 and have the flashcard **Y y** ready.

Lesson

Show the **Y y** flashcard and say its sound. You may want to explain in this lesson that **y** is a consonant at the beginning of words, but it is a vowel when it is at the end of words. This will be taught in a later lesson. Have your student repeat these sentences after you:

> You should remember **y**our Creator in the days of **y**our youth.
>
> The **y**oung girl made a scarf with **y**ellow **y**arn.
>
> The **y**olk of an egg is **y**ellow.
>
> Yes, **y**ou may play in the **y**ard with **y**our **y**o-**y**o.
>
> Yesterday we ate **y**ogurt on a **y**acht.

Help the student to print these words:

> yes   yak   yet   yum   yam

Complete the page, working the bottom section orally before using a pencil.

Page 25

Purpose

Teach the recognition, sound, and formation of the consonant **x**.

Before class begins

Open to page 25 and have the flashcard **X x** ready.

Lesson

Show the **X x** flashcard and explain that it usually is at the end of words. It has the sound made by saying the sounds of **k** and **s** together as in: bo**x** and mi**x**. Print these words on the board or a paper as you ask the student to read them:

> ax   tax   fix   six   fox
>
> ox   mix   box   wax   fax

Complete the page, working the bottom section orally before using a pencil.

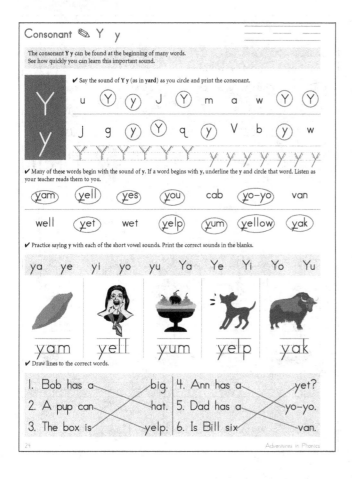

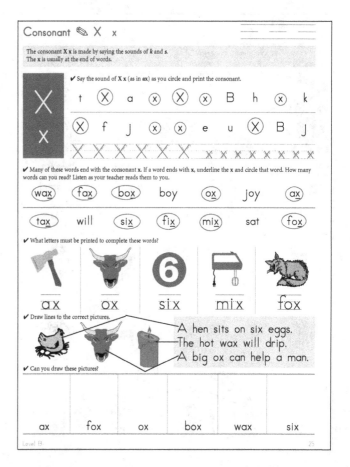

Page 26

Purpose

Teach the recognition, sound, and formation of the consonant **z**.

Before class begins

Open to page 26 and have the flashcard **Z z** ready.

Lesson

Show the **Z z** flashcard and say that it is the sound that a bee makes. We can hear it at the beginning of **z**ag, **z**ig, **z**igzag, **z**oom, and **z**ip code.

Ask these questions:

1. Where can we see many wild animals? (**z**oo)

2. What animal looks like a horse wearing striped pajamas? (**z**ebra)

3. What helps you close up your jacket? (**z**ipper)

4. Who was the short man who was a tax collector and became a Christian? (**Z**acchaeus)

5. What number is like the shape of a circle? (**z**ero)

Help the student print these words:

zap   zip   zest   zag

Have the student complete the page.

Page 27

Purpose

To give practice in reading short vowel words.

Lesson

Help the student to print these words:

at	pen	tip	pop	rub
sat	hen	rip	hop	tub

Discuss the directions and have the student complete the lesson.

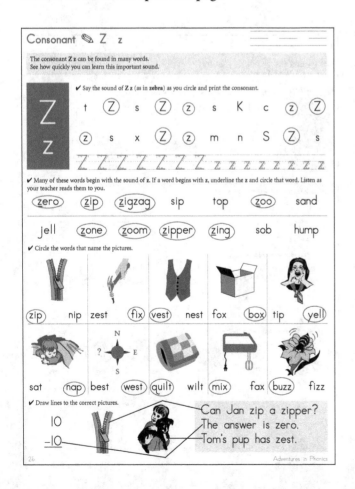

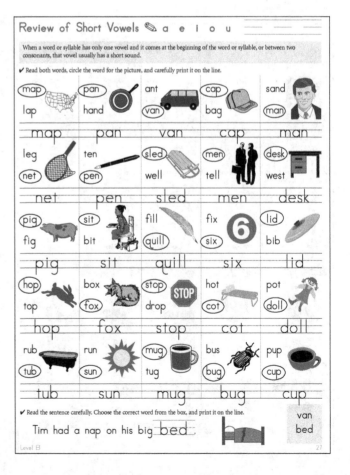

Page 28

Purpose

To give practice in reading and printing short vowel **a** words.

Lesson

Have the student practice reading the list of short vowel **a** words on Charts 1 and 2 (page 215 in the workbook). The student should be able to clearly read Chart 1 before starting on Chart 2. (Chart 2 may be covered at a later time.) It may go slowly at first, but give encouragement and compliments whenever possible.

It would give your student a good introduction and extra practice if you heard him read the lists in the lesson and orally answer the sentences before he does the work independently.

Page 29

Purpose

To give practice in reading and printing short vowel **e** words.

Lesson

Have the student practice reading the list of short vowel **e** words on Chart 3 (page 215 in the workbook). Do not be impatient if it goes slowly at first. Try to give encouragement and compliments whenever possible.

Listen to the student read the lists in the lesson and orally answer the sentences before he does the work independently.

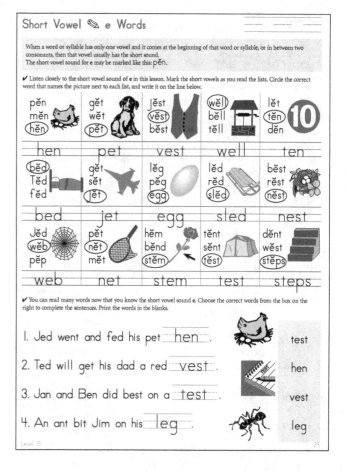

Page 30

Purpose

To give practice in reading and printing short vowel **i** words.

Lesson

Have the student practice reading the list of short vowel **i** words on Chart 4 (page 216 in the workbook). Be patient as you listen. Give encouragement and compliments.

To give your student extra practice, listen to him read the lists in the lesson and orally answer the sentences before he does the work independently.

Page 31

Purpose

To give practice in reading and printing short vowel **o** words.

Lesson

Have the student practice reading the list of short vowel **o** words on Chart 5 (page 216 in the workbook). Patiently listen as you encourage and commend.

To give your student extra practice, listen to him read the lists in the lesson and orally answer the sentences before he does the work independently.

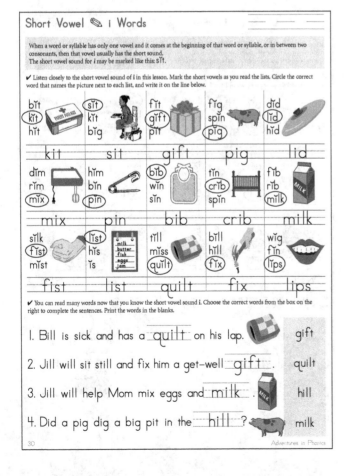

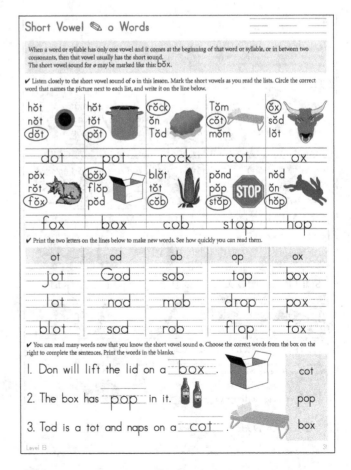

Page 32

Purpose

To give practice in reading and printing short vowel **u** words. To learn about the vowel **o** sometimes having the short vowel **u** sound.

Lesson

Have the student practice reading the list of short vowel **u** words on Chart 6 (page 216 in the workbook). Patiently listen as you encourage and commend.

Introduce the short sound of **u** that is made by the vowel **o**, as in m**o**ther, s**o**n, br**o**ther, etc. Listen and help as your student reads the words on Chart 18 (page 220 in the workbook).

Listen as your student reads the lists in the lesson and orally answers the sentences before he does the work independently.

Page 33

Purpose

To teach words beginning and ending with consonant blends. To cause the student to notice two or three consonants sounding or blending together.

Lesson

Print the following blends and words on the board or paper and listen to your student say them. You may choose to have them read from this key. These are just some of the blends.

bl nd	fl	gl	pl nt
blend	flag	glass	plant
sl pt	ft	cr st	gr sp
slept	gift	crust	grasp
scr	sq(u)	str	lk
scrub	squid	strap	milk

Discuss the lesson orally before it is completed independently.

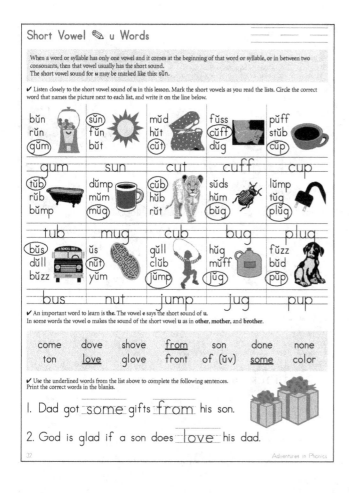

Page 34

Purpose

To teach that in short vowel words, usually the ending consonants **s**, **l**, **f**, and **z** will be *doubled*.

Lesson

Print the following words on the board or paper and listen to your student say them. You may choose to have them read from this key.

grass	bell	fizz	buzz
glass	mess	doll	cuff

Listen as your student gives the answers to the lesson orally before he completes it independently.

Page 35

Purpose

To teach that in short vowel words ending with the **k** sound, that sound is made with **ck**.

Lesson

Print the following words on the board or paper and listen to your student say them. You may choose to have them read from this key.

sack	neck	sock	cluck
crack	pick	flock	back
peck	stick	duck	kick

Have your student read the **ck** words on Chart 7 (page 217 in the workbook).

Listen as he gives the answers to the lesson orally before completing it independently.

Page 36

Purpose

To teach the sounds made by the letters **ng** and **nk** at the end of short vowel words.

Lesson

Print the following words on the board or paper and listen closely to hear if your student says them correctly. You may choose to have them read from this key.

bang	sing	trunk	blank
sang	sung	dunk	sank

Listen as your student reads all the words on the lists and gives the answers to the lesson orally before he completes it independently.

Page 37

Purpose

To review short vowel words that end with **ss**, **ll**, **ff**, **zz**, and **ck**.

Lesson

Have your student read Chart 7 (page 217 in the workbook) with short vowel words ending with **ck**, and review the rule regarding the ending consonants **ss**, **ll**, **ff**, and **zz**. These words can be found on the short vowel Charts 2, 3, 4, and 6 (pages 215 and 216 in the workbook). Is he able to read the words quickly? Maybe he needs to try again at a later time.

Listen as your student reads the sentences and words on the lists and gives the answers to the lesson orally before he completes it independently.

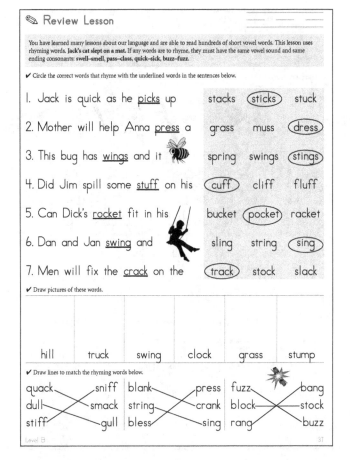

Page 38

Purpose

To teach words with sounds made by the digraphs **sh** and **ch**.

Lesson

Print the following words on the board or paper and listen closely to hear if your student says them correctly. You may choose to have them read from this key.

		sh		
ship	shell	shed	rash	fish

		ch		
chip	chap	chin	lunch	such

Practice reading the words with the digraphs **sh** and **ch** on Chart 8 (page 217 in the workbook). Also, you may want to use the flashcards for these digraphs.

Listen as your student reads all of the words on the lists and gives the answers to the lesson orally before he completes it independently.

Page 39

Purpose

To teach words with the digraphs **th** and **wh**.

Lesson

Print the following words on the board or paper and listen closely to hear if your student says them correctly. You may choose to have them read from this key.

The digraph **th** has two sounds:

	th as in <u>this</u>			
then	that	than	them	the

	th as in <u>thin</u>			
think	thick	Beth	math	bath

	wh as in <u>whip</u>			
when	whip	what	whim	why

Practice reading the **th** and **wh** words on Chart 9 (page 217 in the workbook). Also, you may want to use the flashcards for these digraphs.

Listen as your student reads all of the words on the lists and gives the answers to the lesson orally before he completes it independently.

Consonant Digraphs ✎ sh ch

A consonant digraph has two consonants that make one sound. They may be at the beginning or ending of a word. Two of the digraphs are: **sh** as in **ship** and **ch** as in **chin**.

✔ Underline the digraphs **sh** and **ch** as you read these short vowel words. Circle the correct word that names the picture next to each list, and write it on the line below.

branch / ranch / chip	such / shell / shop	rush / crush / brush	chap / check / chuck	smash / ship / splash
branch	shell	brush	check	ship
shed / shelf / shin	fish / wish / sash	dash / dish / blush	ranch / bunch / chin	chick / chat / chop
shelf	fish	dish	chin	chick

✔ Add these digraphs to the blanks below to make new words. See how quickly you can read the words.

sh		ch		tch	
shock	smash	chap	ranch	catch	pitch
shut	crash	chunk	pinch	hitch	batch
shack	blush	chess	punch	Dutch	match

✔ Choose the words with digraphs **sh** or **ch** from the box on the right to complete these sentences. Print the correct words in the blanks.

1. Mitch has a fresh plum in his <u>lunch</u> .
2. Ashley <u>shut</u> the lid on the box of shells.
3. A little <u>chick</u> sat on a bench in the shed.

shut
chick
lunch

38   Adventures in Phonics

Consonant Digraphs ✎ th wh

Remember this RULE: A consonant digraph has *two* consonants that make *one* sound.
The digraph **th** has two sounds: the hard <u>th</u> sound as in **the** or the soft **th** sound as in **think**.
Learn the digraph **wh** as in **whip**.

✔ Underline the digraphs **th** and **wh** as you read these short vowel words. Circle the correct word that names the picture next to each list, and write it on the line below. NOTE: the b in **thumb** is silent.

with / bath / thing	thick / thin / this	thump / then / thumb	whistle / whip / when
bath	thick	thumb	whip

✔ Add these digraphs to the blanks below to make new words. See how quickly you can read the words.
NOTE: <u>th</u> refers to the hard **th** sound as in <u>the</u>, and **th** refers to the soft **th** sound as in **think**.

th	th	th	wh
that	other	thin	whiff
than	mother	thick	which
them	brother	thank	when
then	gather	think	whip

✔ Choose the words with digraphs **th** or **wh** from the box on the right to complete these sentences. Print the correct words in the blanks.

1. Let us <u>thank</u> God for blessing us.
2. Tim is glad that his <u>mother</u> loves him.
3. <u>Which</u> path is the best?
4. Josh will <u>gather</u> flowers for his mother.

mother
thank
gather
Which

Level B   39

Page 40

Purpose

To teach the long vowel sound of **a**.

Lesson

Be familiar with the directions on the workbook page as you explain the difference between a short vowel sound and a long vowel sound. By now the student should know the main five vowels—**a**, **e**, **i**, **o**, and **u**. Say the long vowel rule several times, having it repeated after you say it.

Study the long vowel **a** words on Charts 10 and 11 (page 218 in the workbook), perhaps reading Chart 10 with this lesson and Chart 11 with the next lesson. Also use the long vowel **a** flashcard.

Give special attention to the first exercise, which compares the short and long vowel words.

Listen as your student reads all of the words on the lists and gives the answers to the lesson orally before he completes it independently.

Some lessons may take a longer time than others, but it is important that the student understands what is being taught. It is better that a second day be spent on a lesson, if there is uncertainty, than to go on and become more confused.

Page 41

Purpose

To teach the long vowel sound of **a**.

Lesson

Review the directions on the workbook page as you discuss the difference between a short vowel sound and a long vowel sound. Does the student remember the long vowel rule? Say it several times, having it repeated after you say it.

Study the rest of the long vowel **a** words on Chart 11 (page 218 in the workbook) or review both Charts 10 and 11 if the student knows them from the previous lesson. Also use the long vowel **a** flashcard.

Listen as your student reads all of the words on the lists and gives the answers to the lesson orally before he completes it independently.

Workbook page 40

Long Vowel ✎ A a

Remember this RULE: When there is only *one* vowel at the beginning or in the middle of a word, it usually has a short sound. This lesson begins teaching the **long vowel rule**.
Remember this RULE: When *two* vowels are in a word, usually the first vowel says its name and the second vowel is silent: ai as in rāin, a_e as in cāke, ay as in prāy.

✔ Practice saying these short vowel words with the long vowel words.
NOTE: the b in lamb is silent.

ai a e ay	ran	rain	can	cane	hat	hate
	pal	pail	cap	cape	mad	made
	bat	bait	Sam	same	pad	paid
	pan	pain	lamb	lame	man	main

✔ Mark the *two* vowels as you read these long vowel a words. Circle the correct word that names the picture next to each list, and write it on the line below.

sāil nāil tāil	cāke tāke māke	vāil hāil pāil	tāpe cāpe āpe	cāme nāme gāme
nail	cake	pail	tape	game
quāil trāil māil	brāin trāin pāin	vāne pāne māne	fāil sāil vāil	stāin rāin māin
mail	train	vane	sail	rain

✔ From the box on the right, choose words that rhyme with the underlined words in these sentences. Print the correct words in the blanks.

1. God made the quail and the little ___snail___.　snail

2. Jake will help his mother bake a ___cake___.　tame

3. Wag is the name of the pet that is ___tame___.　cake

40　　　Adventures in Phonics

Workbook page 41

Long Vowel ✎ A a

Remember the long vowel RULE: When *two* vowels are in a word, usually the first vowel says its name and the second vowel is silent. The letter y is a vowel when it is at the end of a word or syllable. It is silent in the following ay words.

✔ Practice saying these ay words.

pray	lay	hay	ray	clay
bay	may	stay	way	sway
say	jay	pay	gray	stray

✔ Mark the vowels as you read these long vowel a words. Circle the correct word that names the picture next to each list, and write it on the line below.

plāy dāy prāy	wāke skāte bāke	sāint fāint pāint	wāve sāve pāve	swāy trāy gāy
pray	skate	paint	wave	tray
scāle pāle trāil	fāke lāke quāke	rāke sāke stāke	snāil frāil fāil	Kāy hāy pāy
scale	lake	rake	snail	pay

You have learned that short vowels are marked like this: Bŏb's pĕt hăd a băth in a tŭb.
Long vowel words are marked like this: Jāke tākes a trāin in Māy.

✔ In the box below, mark the long vowel words as shown above. Choose words from this list to complete the following sentences. Print the correct words in the blanks.

| dāy | fāint | plāy | trāin |

1. Ann may ___faint___ if a snake came on the trail.

2. God made this ___day___, and Ray is glad.

3. Jay will ___play___ with his gray ___train___.

Level B　　　41

Page 42

Purpose

To teach the long vowel sound of **e**.

Lesson

Be familiar with the directions on the workbook page as you explain the difference between a short vowel sound and a long vowel sound. Say the long vowel rule several times, having it repeated after you say it.

Study the long vowel **e** words on Charts 12 and 13 (pages 218 and 219 in the workbook), perhaps reading Chart 12 with this lesson and Chart 13 with the next lesson. Also use the long vowel **e** flashcard.

Give special attention to the first exercise, which compares the short and long vowel words.

Listen as your student reads all of the words on the lists and gives the answers to the lesson orally before he completes it independently.

Page 43

Purpose

To teach the long vowel sound of **e**.

Lesson

Review the directions on the workbook page as you explain the difference between a short vowel sound and a long vowel sound. Discuss the long vowel rule, asking the student to tell it to you.

Study the rest of the long vowel **e** words on Chart 13 or review both Charts 12 and 13 (pages 218 and 219 in the workbook) if the student knows them from the previous lesson. Also use the long vowel **e** flashcard.

Listen as your student reads all of the words on the lists and gives the answers to the lesson orally before he completes it independently.

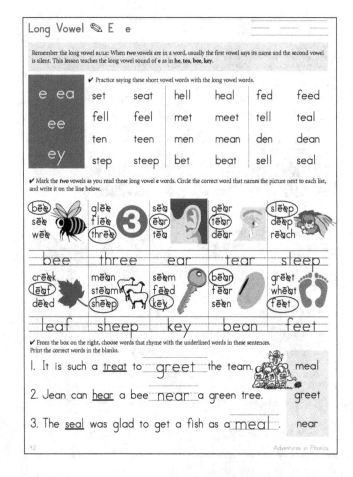

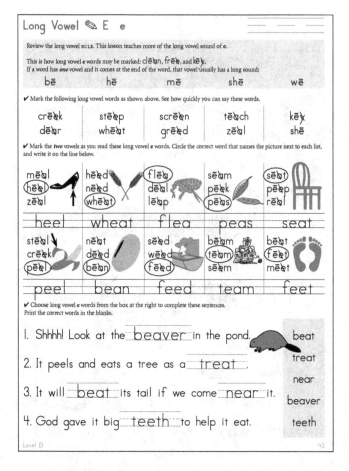

Page 44

Purpose

To teach the long vowel sound of **i**.

Lesson

Be familiar with the directions on the workbook page as you explain the difference between a short vowel sound and a long vowel sound. Say the long vowel rule several times, having it repeated after you say it.

Study the long vowel **i** words on Charts 14 and 15 (page 219 in the workbook), perhaps reading Chart 14 with this lesson and Chart 15 with the next lesson. Also use the long vowel **i** flashcard.

Give special attention to the first exercise, which compares the short and long vowel words.

Listen as your student reads all of the words on the lists and gives the answers to the lesson orally before he completes it independently.

Page 45

Purpose

To teach the long vowel sound of **i**.

Lesson

Review the directions on the workbook page as you explain the difference between a short vowel sound and a long vowel sound. Discuss the long vowel rule, asking the student to say it to you.

Study the rest of the long vowel **i** words on Chart 15 (page 219 in the workbook) or review both Charts 14 and 15 if the student knows them from the previous lesson. Also use the long vowel **i** flashcard.

Listen as your student reads all of the words on the lists and gives the answers to the lesson orally before he completes it independently.

Note that the **s** can make the **z** sound in some words. Explain to your student that the **s** in ri**s**e and wi**s**e makes the sound of **z**.

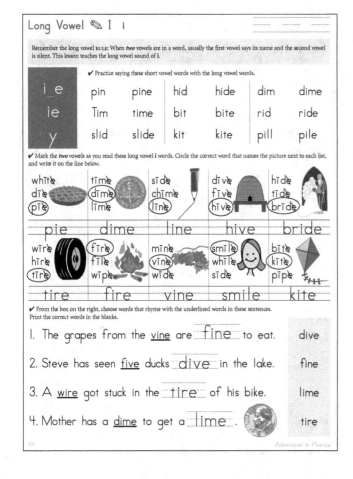

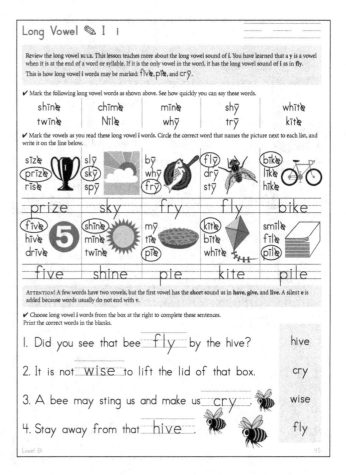

Page 46

Purpose

To teach the long vowel sound of **o**.

Lesson

Be familiar with the directions on the workbook page as you explain the difference between a short vowel sound and a long vowel sound. Say the long vowel rule several times, having it repeated after you say it.

Study the long vowel **o** words on Charts 16 and 17 (page 220 in the workbook), perhaps reading Chart 16 with this lesson and Chart 17 with the next lesson. Also use the long vowel **o** flashcard.

Give special attention to the first exercise, which compares the short and long vowel words.

Listen as your student reads all of the words on the lists and gives the answers to the lesson orally before he completes it independently.

Note that the **s** can make the **z** sound in some words. Explain to your student that the **s** in po**s**e, ro**s**e, cho**s**e, and no**s**e makes the sound of **z**.

Page 47

Purpose

To teach the long vowel sound of **o**.

Lesson

Review the directions on the workbook page as you explain the difference between a short vowel sound and a long vowel sound. Discuss the long vowel rule, asking the student to say it to you.

Study the rest of the long vowel **o** words on Chart 17 (page 220 in the workbook) or review both Charts 16 and 17 if the student knows them from the previous lesson. Also use the long vowel **o** flashcard.

Listen as your student reads all of the words on the lists and gives the answers to the lesson orally before he completes it independently.

Note that the **s** can make the **z** sound in some words. Explain to your student that the **s** in po**s**e, ro**s**e, cho**s**e, and no**s**e makes the sound of **z**.

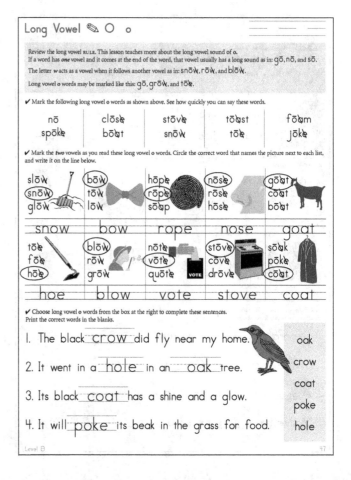

Page 48

Purpose

To teach the long vowel sound of **u**.

Lesson

Be familiar with the directions on the workbook page as you explain the difference between a short vowel sound and a long vowel sound. Say the long vowel rule several times, having it repeated after you say it.

Study the long vowel **u** words on Chart 19 (page 221 in the workbook), perhaps reading half of them with this lesson and the other half with the next lesson. Also use the long vowel **u** flashcard.

Give special attention to the first exercise, which compares the short and long vowel words.

Listen as your student reads all of the words on the lists and gives the answers to the lesson orally before he completes it independently.

Note that the **s** can make the **z** sound in some words. Explain to your student that the **s** in use and fuse makes the sound of **z**.

Page 49

Purpose

To teach the long vowel sound of **u**.

Lesson

Review the directions on the workbook page as you explain the difference between a short vowel sound and a long vowel sound. Discuss the long vowel rule, asking the student to say it to you.

Study the rest of the long vowel **u** words on Chart 19 (page 221 in the workbook). Also use the long vowel **u** flashcard.

Listen as your student reads all of the words on the lists and gives the answers to the lesson orally before he completes it independently.

Note that the **s** can make the **z** sound in some words. Explain to your student that the **s** in u**s**e makes the sound of **z**.

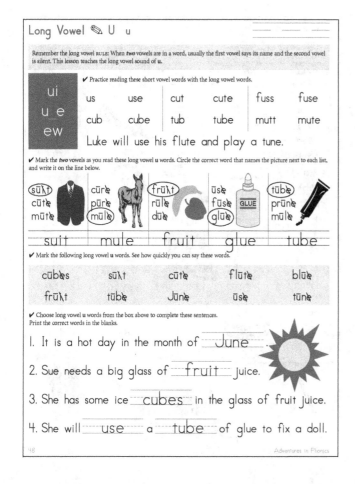

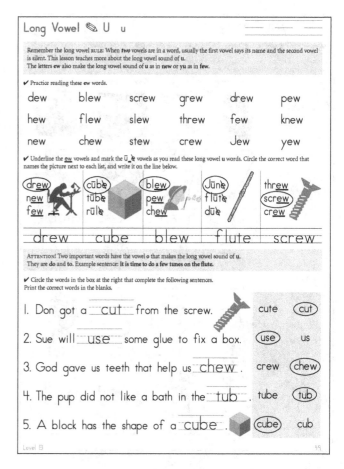

Page 50

Purpose

To review words that have long or short vowels.

Lesson

Say the long vowel rule, having it repeated after you say it.

Read all of the long vowel **a** words on Charts 10 and 11 (page 218 in the workbook).

Review the short vowel sounds **a, e, i, o, u**, with special attention to the short vowel **a**. Do you remember the rule that says there is only *one* vowel in short vowel words?

Listen as your student reads the words on the list and gives the answers to the lesson orally before he completes it independently.

Page 51

Purpose

To review words that have long or short vowels.

Lesson

Say the long vowel rule, having it repeated after you say it.

Read all of the long vowel **e** words on Charts 12 and 13 (pages 218 and 219 in the workbook).

Review the short vowel sounds **a, e, i, o, u**, with special attention to the short vowel **e**. Review the rule that says there is only *one* vowel in short vowel words.

Listen as your student reads the words on the list and gives the answers to the lesson orally before he completes it independently.

Page 52

Purpose

To review words that have long or short vowels.

Lesson

Say the long vowel rule, having it repeated after you say it. Read all of the long vowel **i** and **u** words on Charts 14 and 15 (page 219 in the workbook), and Chart 19 (page 221).

To give practice on what the lesson includes, print the following boxes on the board or paper and ask your student to use them as guides and print the words under the correct column as you pronounce them one at a time.

a_e	ee	i_e	o_e	u_e	ay
free	cone	way	cake	tube	
cute	mine	tape	pray	rose	
take	feet	tune	kite	tree	

For more words, refer to the long vowel charts.

Review the short vowel rule and short vowel **i** sound before doing the bottom exercise.

Check the words and have the student correct any errors as soon as he completes the lesson.

Page 53

Purpose

To review words that have long or short vowels.

Lesson

Say the long vowel rule, having it repeated after you say it. Read the long vowel o words on Charts 16 and 17 (page 220 in the workbook).

To help introduce the lesson, put the following boxes on the board or paper and have your student say them until you feel that he knows them. Print the words and have him circle the vowel sounds he sees in each word before he reads the word.

ui	ai	oa	ea	ew	ow
heat	coat	few	soap	pail	
slow	suit	meal	flow	seal	
new	fail	main	chew	toad	

If you want to add more words, refer to the long vowel charts.

Review the short vowel rule and short vowel **o** sound before doing the bottom exercise.

Check the work and have the student correct any errors as soon as he completes the lesson.

Page 54

Purpose

To teach the rule that a single **i** usually is short, except when followed by **ld**, **nd**, and **gh**. The **gh** is silent. To review short vowel words ending with **ck**.

Lesson

Ask the student to read the words on Chart 21 (page 221 in the workbook). Review the rule on Chart 7 (page 217 in the workbook) about short vowel words ending with the **ck**.

Listen as the student reads all of the words on the lists in the lesson and gives the answers to the lesson orally before he completes it independently.

Page 55

Purpose

To teach the rule that a single **o** may have the long vowel sound when followed by two consonants such as **ld**, **st**, **th**, **ll**, and **lt**. To review short vowel words ending with double consonants **ff**, **ll**, **ss**, and **zz**.

Lesson

Ask the student to read the words on Chart 22 (page 222 in the workbook). Review the rule about doubling the consonants **ff**, **ll**, **ss**, and **zz** at the end of short vowel words.

Listen as the student reads all of the words on the lists and gives the answers to the lesson orally before he completes it independently.

Page 56

Purpose

To teach the sound of **ow** and **ou** as in the words <u>c</u><u>ow</u> and h<u>ou</u><u>se</u>.

Lesson

If this is the first lesson about the **ow** and **ou** that the student has had, spend as much time as needed for teaching it. Help him read the words from Charts 23 and 24 (page 222 in the workbook), perhaps reading words from Chart 23 for this lesson, and the rest from Chart 24 for the next lesson. Also use the **ow/ou** flashcard.

Listen as the student reads all of the words on the lists and gives the answers to the lesson orally before he completes it independently.

Page 57

Purpose

To teach the sound of **ow** and **ou** as in the words <u>c</u><u>ow</u> and h<u>ou</u><u>se</u>.

Lesson

Review the sound of **ow** and **ou**. Help the student read the rest of the words that were not read from Chart 24 (page 222 in the workbook). Repetition greatly helps to confirm any lesson. Use drills whenever it is necessary for strengthening reading skills. Also use the **ow/ou** flashcard.

Listen as the student reads all of the words on the lists and gives the answers to the lesson orally before he completes it independently.

Page 58

Purpose

To teach the sound of **oi** and **oy** as in the words c<u>oi</u>n and j<u>oy</u>.

Lesson

If this is the first lesson about the **oi** and **oy** that the student has had, spend as much time as needed for teaching it. Help him to read the words from Chart 25 (page 223 in the workbook). Also use the **oi/oy** flashcard.

Listen as the student reads all of the words on the lists and gives the answers to the lesson orally before he completes it independently.

Page 59

Purpose

To teach the sound of **oi** and **oy** as in the words c<u>oi</u>n and j<u>oy</u>.

Lesson

Listen as your student again reads the words from Chart 25 (page 223 in the workbook). Also use the **oi/oy** flashcard.

Prepare for the first part of the lesson by teaching that **oi** is usually followed by another consonant or two, but the **oy** usually is at the end of a word or syllable.

Have the student give the answers to the lesson orally before he completes the page independently.

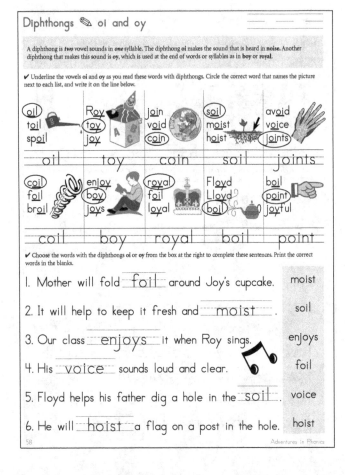

Page 60

Purpose

To teach the sound of **oo** as in the word <u>zoo</u>.

Lesson

If this is the first lesson about the vowel digraph **oo** that the student has had, spend as much time as needed for teaching it. Help him to read the words from Charts 26 and 27 (page 223 in the workbook). It may be fun if you read one word and your student reads the next word, etc. It is important for him to know the words, so it is worth spending the time. Also use the **oo** flashcard.

Listen as the student reads all of the words on the lists and gives the answers to the lesson orally before he completes it independently.

Page 61

Purpose

To teach the sound of **oo** as in the word <u>book</u>.

Lesson

Teach the second sound that the vowel digraph **oo** makes as well as other vowels that make that sound. Spend as much time as necessary. Help your student to read the words found in the first four columns of Chart 28 (page 224 in the workbook). Also use the **oo** flashcard as in **book**.

Emphasize that at times **o, u,** and **ou** can also make the sound of **oo** as in **book**. Help him to read the words found on Chart 18 and in the last two columns on chart 28.

Listen as the student reads all of the words on the lists and gives the answers to the lesson orally before he completes it independently.

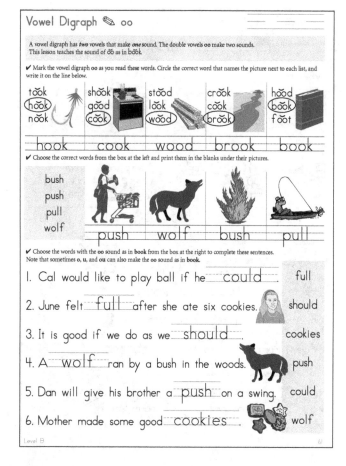

Page 62

Purpose

To teach the sound of **ar** as in the word a<u>r</u>k.

Lesson

If this is the first lesson about the **ar** sound that the student has had, spend as much time as needed for teaching it. Help him to read the words from Charts 29 and 30 (page 224 in the workbook). Also use the **är** flashcard.

Listen as the student reads all of the words on the lists and gives the answers to the lesson orally before he completes it independently.

Page 63

Purpose

To teach the sound of **or** as in the word <u>cor</u>n.

Lesson

If this is the first lesson about the sound of **or** that the student has had, spend as much time as needed for teaching it. Help him to read the words from Chart 31 (page 225 in the workbook). Also use the **ôr** flashcard.

Listen as the student reads all of the words on the lists and gives the answers to the lesson orally before he completes it independently.

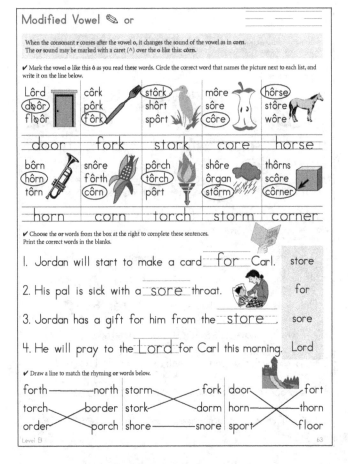

Page 64

Purpose

To teach the sound of **er** as in the words <u>ve</u>rse, <u>gir</u>l, and ch<u>ur</u>ch.

Lesson

Carefully teach this sound with the three sets of letters **er**, **ir**, and **ur**. Help your student to read the words on Chart 32 and the first three columns on Chart 33 (page 225 in the workbook). Also use the **er** flashcard.

Listen as the student reads all of the words on the lists and gives the answers to the lesson orally before he completes it independently.

Page 65

Purpose

To teach the sound of **er** as in the words <u>ear</u>th and (w)<u>or</u>ld.

Lesson

If this is the first lesson about the **er** sound spelled with **ear** and **(w)or** that the student has had, spend as much time as needed for teaching it. Help him to read the words in the last three columns on Chart 33 (page 225 in the workbook). Also use the **er** flashcard.

Listen as the student reads all of the words on the lists and gives the answers to the lesson orally before he completes it independently.

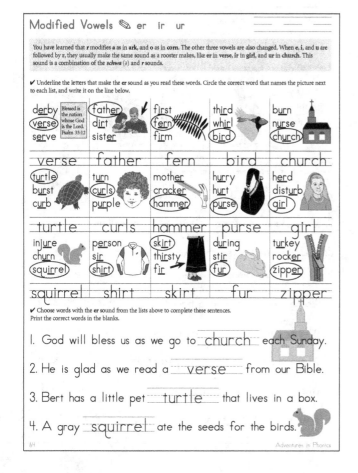

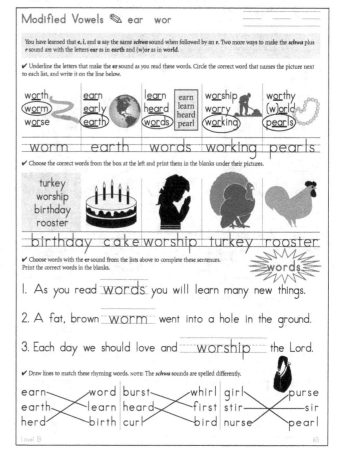

Page 66

Purpose

To teach the sound of **ar** as in the word squ<u>are</u>.

Lesson

Carefully teach your student the seven sets of letters that can have the **âr** sound. Help him to read the words from Chart 34 (page 226 in the workbook). Also use the **âr** flashcard; note that the word **their** is also listed on Chart 34 as another spelling for the **âr** sound, but it is not covered in this lesson.

Listen as the student reads all of the words on the lists and gives the answers to the lesson orally before he completes it independently.

Note that the answers in sentence #3 may be written in any order.

Page 67

Purpose

To teach the sound of **ar** as in the word squ<u>are</u>.

Lesson

Review the six sets of letters that can have the **âr** sound. Listen as your student again reads the words from Chart 34 (page 226 in the workbook). Also use the **âr** flashcard; note that the word **their** is also listed on Chart 34 as another spelling for the **âr** sound, but it is not covered in this lesson.

Have the student give the answers to the lesson orally before he completes it independently.

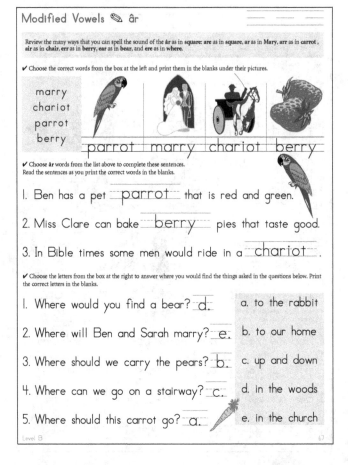

Page 68

Purpose

To teach the sound of **ô** as in the words **d<u>o</u>g**, **b<u>al</u>l**, **<u>saw</u>**, and **h<u>au</u>l**.

Lesson

Carefully teach the four sets of letters that can have the **ô** sound. Help your student to read the words in Chart 35 and the first four lists on Chart 36 (page 226 in the workbook). This may take some time, but patient encouragement will be most beneficial. Also use the **ô** flashcard.

Listen as the student reads all of the words on the lists and gives the answers to the lesson orally before he completes it independently.

Page 69

Purpose

To continue to teach the sound of **ô** that is found in the words **d<u>augh</u>ter** and **b<u>ough</u>t**.

Lesson

Review the six sets of letters that can make the **ô** sound. Mention that the letters gh are silent in these words.

o	al	aw
au	augh	ough

Listen as he again reads the words from last two columns on Chart 36 (page 226 in the workbook).

Have the student give the answers to the lesson orally before he completes it independently.

Page 70

Purpose

To review the sounds of **oo**, **oo**, **ou**, **ow**, **oi**, and **oy**.

Lesson

Print these letters on the board or paper and have your student say them to you.

o͞o	o͝o	ou	ow	oi	oy

Print these words on the board or paper and ask him to circle one of the above sounds that is in each word. Have him pronounce the word.

moist	tool	enjoy	sound
round	crowd	joint	roost
joy	good	power	shook

You may want to show and discuss the charts of words with these sounds.

Check your student's answers and have him correct any errors as soon as the lesson is completed.

Page 71

Purpose

To review the sounds of ar, or, er, ir, ur, ear, (w)or.

Lesson

Print these letters on the board or paper and have your student say them to you.

ar	or	er	ir
ur	ear	(w)or	

Print the following words on the board or paper and ask your student to circle one of the above sounds that is in the word. Have him pronounce the word.

hurt	verse	horn	star
bird	word	turn	earn
barn	earth	shirt	corn

Have the student read the list of words orally before he completes the page independently.

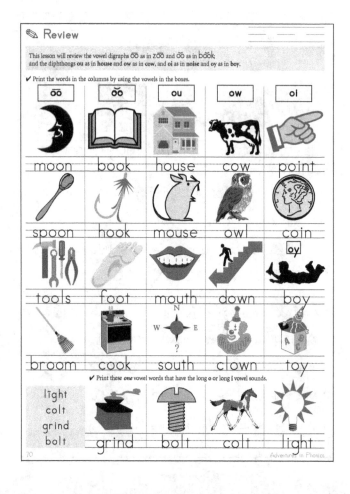

Page 72

Purpose

To review the sets of letters that make the sounds of **âr** as in **square** and **ô** as in **dog**.

Lesson

Have your student look at the various ways of spelling the **âr** sound as they are printed on Chart 34 (page 226 in the workbook). Listen to him read the words. It may be best if the work on the top half of the lesson were completed at this time.

Next discuss the sets of letters that are ways of spelling the **ô** sound as they are printed on Charts 35 and 36 (page 226 in the workbook). If you feel the lists would be too much for him to read, it may go better if you read every other word alternately with him.

After you have heard your student read the lesson, have him complete it independently.

Page 73

Purpose

To review the three sounds of **ear**.

Lesson

Print these letters on the board or paper and review the sounds with your student.

$$\bar{e}\!\!\;\!\!\,r \qquad \dot{e}\,\!\!\;r \qquad \hat{e}\hat{a}r$$

Spend sufficient time reading the first three lines and the list of words in the lesson.

After the page has been completed orally, the student may complete it independently.

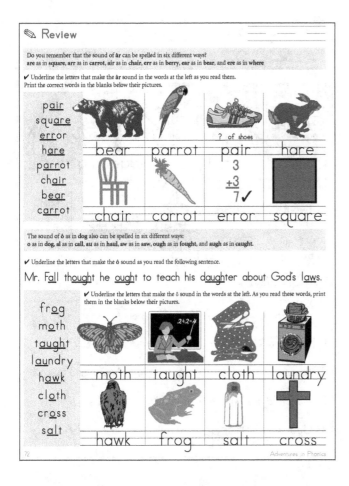

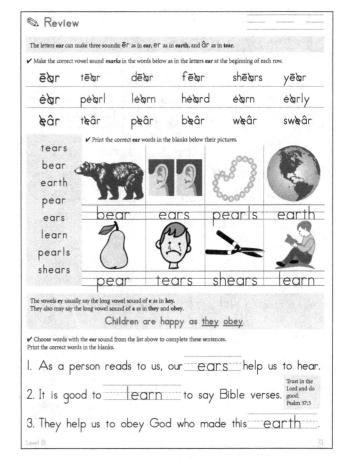

Page 74

Purpose

To teach the soft sound of **c**.

Lesson

Listen to your student read the list of words on Chart 37 (page 227 in the workbook).

When you feel that your student knows the words well, have him give the answers orally before completing the page independently.

Page 75

Purpose

To teach the soft sound of **g**.

Lesson

Listen to your student read the list of words on Chart 38 (page 227 in the workbook).

When you feel that he knows the words well, have your student give the answers orally before completing the page independently.

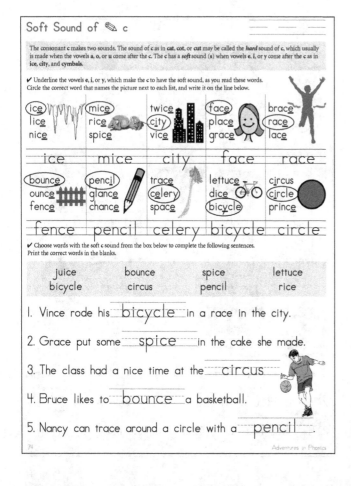

Page 76

Purpose

To teach the consonant digraphs **kn** and **wr**.

Lesson

After you have discussed these digraphs with your student, have him read the words in the first five columns on Chart 42 (page 228 in the workbook) until he can say them quickly. Also use the **kn** and **wr** flashcards.

After you have heard your student read the lesson, have him complete it independently.

Page 77

Purpose

To teach the sounds of sets of letters with silent consonants or vowels.

Lesson

Study the sets of sounds at the top of the lesson page. Spend as much time as necessary to listen to your student work his way through the entire lesson orally. Encourage him to do his work carefully.

When you feel that he knows the words well, have your student complete the page independently.

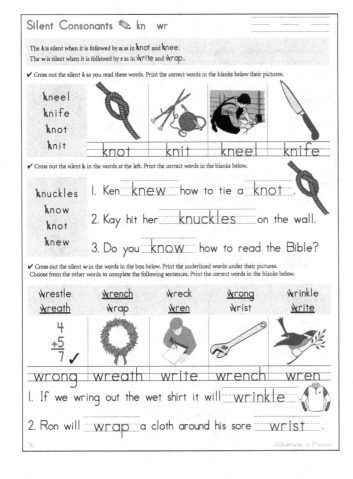

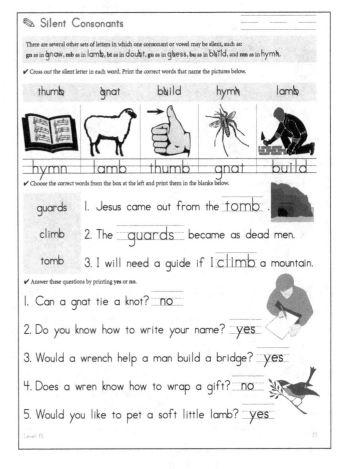

Page 78

Purpose

To teach the short vowel **e** sound of **ea**.

Lesson

Listen to your student read the list of words on Chart 39 (page 227 in the workbook). Discuss words that rhyme, mentioning that words must have the same vowel sounds and ending sounds. Say these words to train him to hear the matching vowel sounds:

care	rare	night	flight
lace	face	dead	head
raw	thaw	stool	pool

When you feel that he knows the words well, have your student give the answers orally before completing the page independently.

Page 79

Purpose

To teach the long vowel **a** sound of **ea** and the long vowel **u** sound of **ou** as in **you**.

Lesson

Listen to your student read the first list of words on Chart 40 (page 228 in the workbook). Discuss all of the sounds **ea** can make:

ē̲a̶ –ear   ĕa̶ –head   ̲eā –steak

Mention that when the consonant **r** follows **ea**, it makes several more sounds. It may be best to complete the top section of the lesson at this time.

Discuss the directions for the middle section, teaching that the **ou** sometimes has the long **u** as in **you** and **through**. When he can read the **ou** words quickly, have your student print the words in the blanks under the correct picture.

Does he understand about rhyming words? Discuss again that the vowel sounds and endings must match in rhyming words.

tame	same	soup	loop
note	goat	weep	keep
hook	took	steak	wake

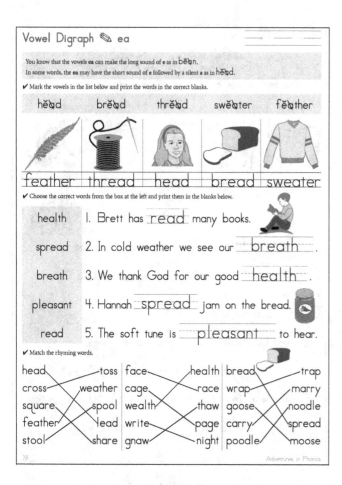

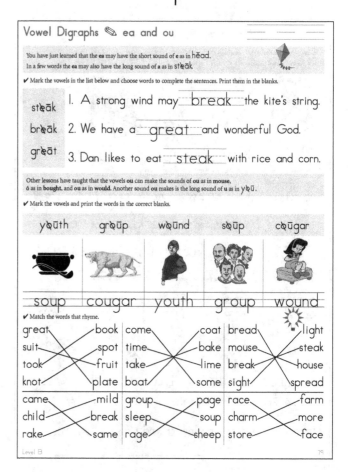

Page 80

Purpose

To teach about compound words.

Lesson

Explain how two special words are put together to form one (*compound*) word as in:

mailbox	doorway	snowman
sailboat	bluebird	pancake

This lesson introduces the student to simple word division; that is, the division of compound words. Have your student divide the words above, as follows:

mail–box	door–way	snow–man
sail–boat	blue–bird	pan–cake

Dividing words by syllables will be introduced later.

Go through the lesson and have the student give the answers orally before completing it independently.

Page 81

Purpose

To teach about compound words.

Lesson

Review how two special words are put together to form one (*compound*) word as in:

rosebud	teapot	highway
notebook	starfish	airport

This lesson also emphasizes simple word division; that is, the division of compound words. Have your student divide the words above, as follows:

rose–bud	tea–pot	high–way
note–book	star–fish	air–port

Discuss the lesson and have the student give the answers orally before completing it independently.

Page 82

Purpose

To review words that are spelled with the short vowel sound of **a**.

Lesson

Listen to your student read the words in Chart 1 (page 215 in the workbook).

If he has no difficulty and can quickly say the words, discuss the lesson and have him answer orally before he completes it independently.

Page 83

Purpose

To review more words that are spelled with the short vowel sound of **a**.

Lesson

Listen to your student read the words in Chart 2 (page 215 in the workbook).

If he has no difficulty and can quickly say the words, discuss the lesson and have him answer orally before he completes it independently.

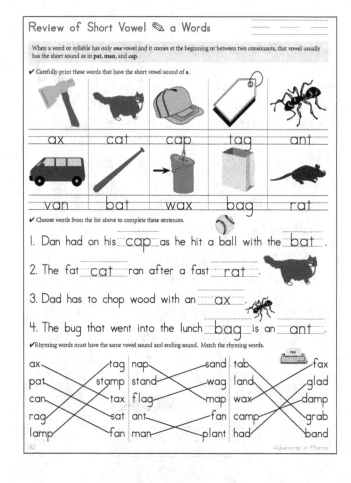

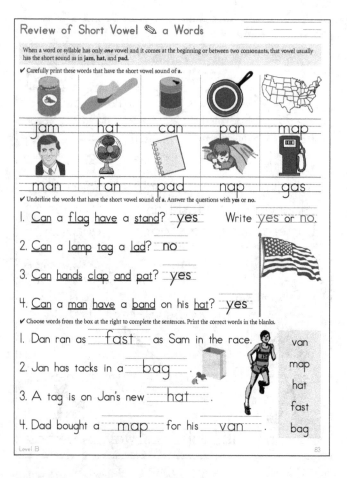

Page 84

Purpose

To review words that are spelled with the short vowel sound of **e**.

Lesson

Listen to your student read the words in Chart 3 (page 215 in the workbook).

If he has no difficulty and can quickly say the words, discuss the lesson and have him answer orally before he completes it independently.

Page 85

Purpose

To review more words that are spelled with the short vowel sound of **e**.

Lesson

Listen to your student read the words in Chart 3.

If he has no difficulty and can quickly say the words, discuss the lesson and have him answer orally before he completes it independently.

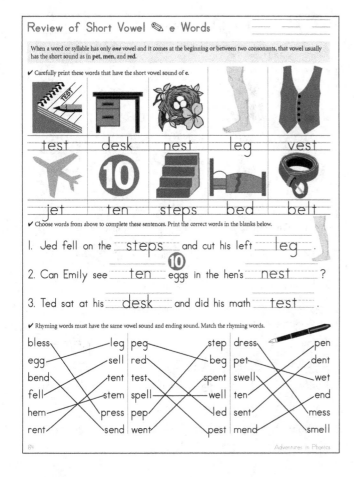

Review of Short Vowel ✎ e Words

When a word or syllable has only *one* vowel and it comes at the beginning or between two consonants, that vowel usually has the short sound as in **pet**, **men**, and **red**.

✔ Carefully print these words that have the short vowel sound of **e**.

test   desk   nest   leg   vest
jet   ten   steps   bed   belt

✔ Choose words from above to complete these sentences. Print the correct words in the blanks below.

1. Jed fell on the _steps_ and cut his left _leg_ .

2. Can Emily see _ten_ ⑩ eggs in the hen's _nest_ ?

3. Ted sat at his _desk_ and did his math _test_ .

✔ Rhyming words must have the same vowel sound and ending sound. Match the rhyming words.

bless   leg
egg   sell
bend   tent
fell   stem
hem   press
rent   send

peg   step
red   beg
test   spent
spell well
pep   ten
went   led
       pest

dress   pen
pet   dent
swell   wet
ten   end
sent   mess
mend   smell

Review of Short Vowel ✎ e Words

When a word or syllable has only *one* vowel and it comes at the beginning or between two consonants, that vowel usually has the short sound as in **bed**, **met**, and **ten**.

✔ Carefully print these words that have the short vowel sound of **e**.

hen   bed   steps   net   west
tent   web   pen   men   vest

✔ You have learned that the vowels **ea** may sometimes have the short sound of **e** as in **head**.
Choose the **ea** words from the box below and print them under their correct pictures.

head   bread   feather   thread   sweater

thread   feather   sweater   bread   head

✔ Complete these sentences with the **ea** words from the list. Print the correct words in the blanks below.

1. It is important to eat _breakfast_ .

2. Ted read the _headline_ of the paper.

3. Ned will _measure_ the size of the hall.

4. We will trust in God _instead_ of worrying.

instead
headline
breakfast
measure

Page 86

Purpose

To review words that are spelled with the short vowel sound of **i**.

Lesson

Listen to your student read the words in Chart 4 (page 216 in the workbook).

If he has no difficulty and can quickly say the words, discuss the lesson and have him answer orally before he completes it independently.

Page 87

Purpose

To review more words that are spelled with the short vowel sound of **i**.

Lesson

Listen to your student read the words in Chart 4.

If he has no difficulty and can quickly say the words, discuss the lesson and have him answer orally before he completes it independently.

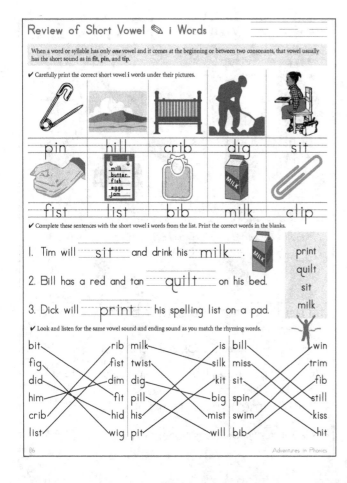

Page 88

Purpose

To review words that are spelled with the short vowel sound of **o**.

Lesson

Listen to your student read the words in Chart 5 (page 216 in the workbook).

If he has no difficulty and can quickly say the words, discuss the lesson and have him answer orally before he completes it independently.

Page 89

Purpose

To review more words that are spelled with the short vowel sound of **o**.

Lesson

Listen to your student read the words in Chart 5.

If he has no difficulty and can quickly say the words, discuss the lesson and have him answer orally before he completes it independently.

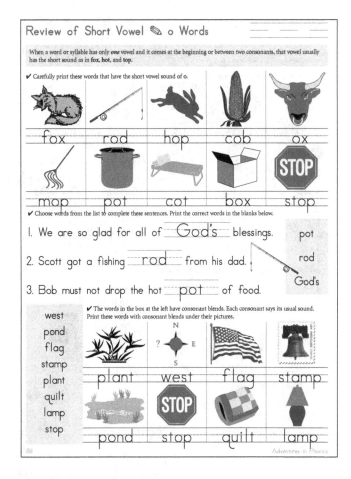

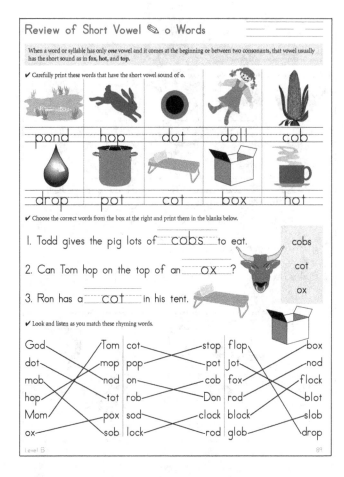

Page 90

Purpose

To review words that are spelled with the short vowel sound of **u**.

Lesson

Listen to your student read the words in Chart 6 (page 216 in the workbook).

If he has no difficulty and can quickly say the words, discuss the lesson and have him answer orally before he completes it independently.

Page 91

Purpose

To review more words that are spelled with the short vowel sound of **u**.

Lesson

Listen to your student read the words in Chart 6. Also have him read Chart 18 (page 220 in the workbook).

If he has no difficulty and can quickly say the words, discuss the lesson and have him answer orally before he completes it independently.

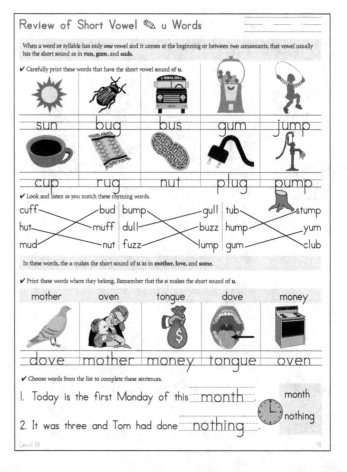

Page 92

Purpose

To review words that are spelled with *double* consonants **ss**, **ff**, **ll**, and **zz**.

Lesson

Look over Charts 2, 3, 4 and 6 (pages 215 and 216 in the workbook) with your student and have him find and read the words that end with these double letters.

If he has no difficulty and can quickly say the words, discuss the lesson and have him answer orally before he completes it independently.

Page 93

Purpose

To review short vowel words that end with **ck**.

Lesson

Listen to your student read the words on Chart 7 (page 217 in the workbook).

If he has no difficulty and can quickly say the words, discuss the lesson and have him answer orally before he completes it independently.

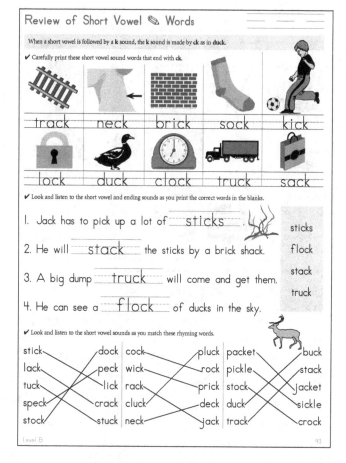

Page 94

Purpose

To review words that are spelled with the long vowel sound of **a**.

Lesson

Listen to your student read the words in Chart 10 (page 218 in the workbook).

If he has no difficulty and can quickly say the words, discuss the lesson and have him answer orally before he completes it independently.

Page 95

Purpose

To review more words that are spelled with the long vowel sound of **a**.

Lesson

Listen to your student read the words in Chart 11 (page 218 in the workbook).

If he has no difficulty and can quickly say the words, discuss the lesson and have him answer orally before he completes it independently.

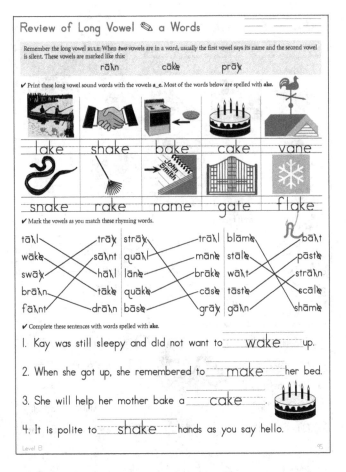

Page 96

Purpose

To review words that are spelled with the long vowel sound of **e**.

Lesson

Listen to your student read the words in Chart 12 (page 218 in the workbook).

If he has no difficulty and can quickly say the words, discuss the lesson and have him answer orally before he completes it independently.

Page 97

Purpose

To review more words that are spelled with the long vowel sound of **e**. To review a few words with the consonant digraph **ch**.

Lesson

Listen to your student read the words in Chart 13 (page 219 in the workbook).

If he has no difficulty and can quickly say the words, discuss the lesson and have him answer orally before he completes it independently.

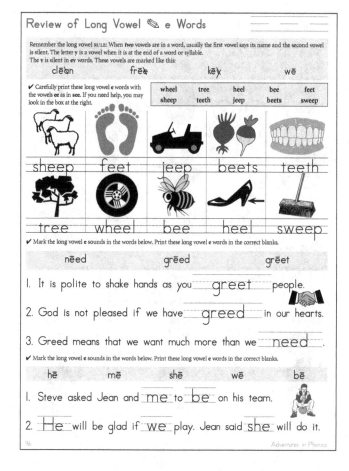

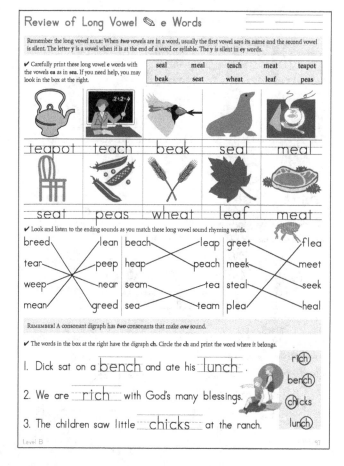

Page 98

Purpose

To review words that are spelled with the long vowel sound of **i**.

Lesson

Listen to your student read the words in Chart 14 (page 219 in the workbook).

If he has no difficulty and can quickly say the words, discuss the lesson and have him answer orally before he completes it independently.

Page 99

Purpose

To review more words that are spelled with the long vowel sound of **i**.

Lesson

Listen to your student read the words in Chart 15 (page 219 in the workbook). Also review the words in Chart 21 (page 221 in the workbook).

If he has no difficulty and can quickly say the words, discuss the lesson and have him answer orally before he completes it independently.

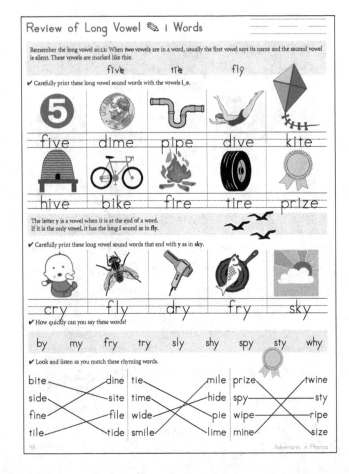

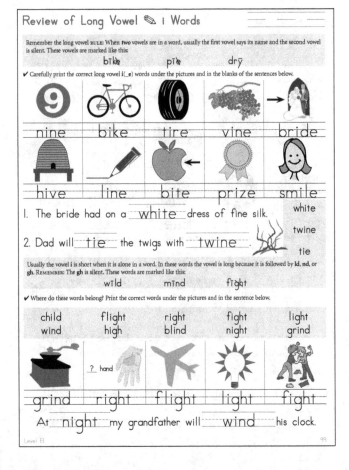

Page 100

Purpose

To review words that are spelled with the long vowel sound of **o**.

Lesson

Listen to your student read the words in Chart 16 (page 220 in the workbook).

If the student has no difficulty and can quickly say the words, discuss the lesson and have him answer orally before he completes it independently.

Page 101

Purpose

To review more words that are spelled with the long vowel sound of **o**.

Lesson

Listen to your student read the words in Chart 17 (page 220 in the workbook). Also have him read the words in Chart 22 (page 222 in the workbook).

If the student has no difficulty and can quickly say the words, discuss the lesson and have him answer orally before he completes it independently.

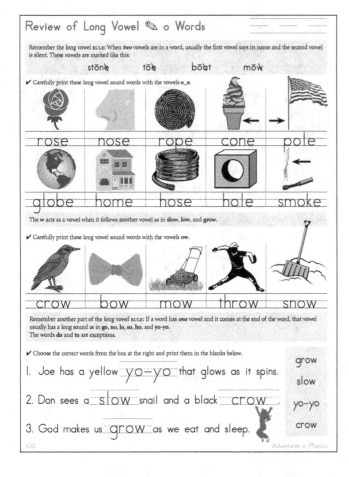

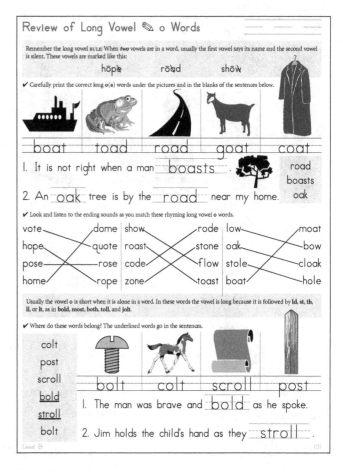

Page 102

Purpose

To review words that are spelled with the long vowel sound of **u**.

Lesson

Listen to your student read the words in Chart 19 (page 221 in the workbook).

If the student has no difficulty and can quickly say the words, discuss the lesson and have him answer orally before he completes it independently.

Page 103

Purpose

To review words that have the long **u** sound and are spelled with **oo**.

Lesson

Listen to your student read the words in Chart 26 (page 223 in the workbook).

If the student has no difficulty and can quickly say the words, discuss the lesson and have him answer orally before he completes it independently.

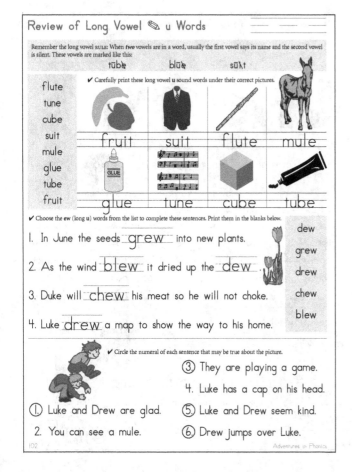

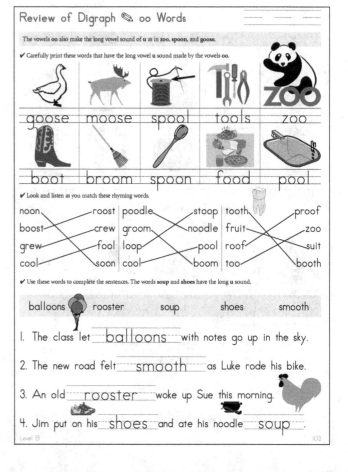

Page 104

Purpose

To review words that are spelled with the sound of **oo** as in **zoo** and **oo** as in **book**.

Lesson

Listen to your student read the words in Chart 27 (page 223 in the workbook) and the first four columns in Chart 28 (page 224 in the workbook).

If the student has no difficulty and can quickly say the words, discuss the lesson and have him answer orally before he completes it independently.

Page 105

Purpose

To review words that are spelled with the sound of **oo** as in **zoo** and **oo** as in **book**.

Lesson

Listen to your student read the words in the last two columns of Chart 28.

If the student has no difficulty and can quickly say the words, discuss the lesson and have him answer orally before he completes it independently.

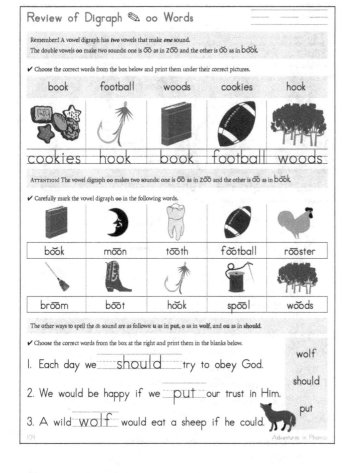

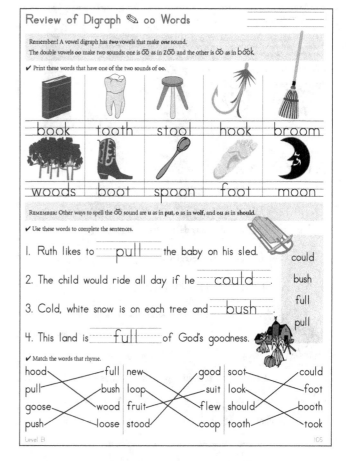

Page 106

Purpose

1. To recall that a *diphthong* is two vowels sounded so that both vowels can be heard blended together as one.

2. To review words that have the diphthong sound of **ou** made by two sets of vowels: **ow** as in **cow** and **ou** as in **house**. Remember that in some words the **ow** has the long **o** sound.

Lesson

Listen to your student read the words in Chart 23 (page 222 in the workbook).

If the student has no difficulty and can quickly say the words, discuss the lesson and have him answer orally before he completes it independently.

Page 107

Purpose

To review words that have the diphthong sound of **ou** made by two sets of vowels: **ow** as in **cow** and **ou** as in **house**. Remember that in some words the **ow** has the long **o** sound.

Lesson

Listen to your student read the words in Chart 24 (page 222 in the workbook).

If the student has no difficulty and can quickly say the words, discuss the lesson and have him answer orally before he completes it independently.

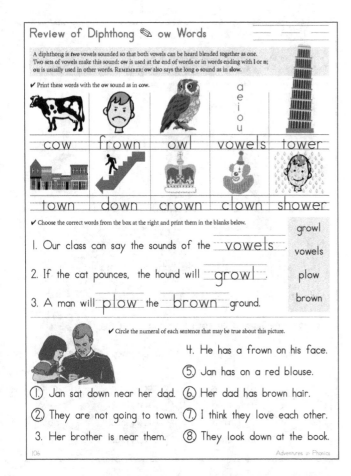

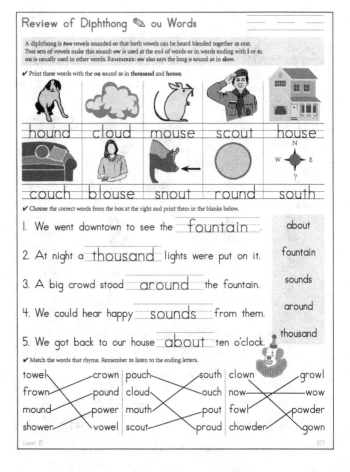

Page 108

Purpose

1. To review words that have the *diphthong* sound of **oi** made by two sets of vowels: **oi** as in **noise** and **oy** as in **boy**.

2. To review the two sounds made by the consonant digraph **th**.

Lesson

Listen to your student read the words in Chart 25 (page 223 in the workbook), as well as the **th** words in Chart 9 (page 217 in the workbook).

If the student has no difficulty and can quickly say the words, discuss the lesson and have him answer orally before he completes it independently.

* Note that the matching exercise at the top of the page may have these alternate answers: *royal* and *spoil* may be matched, and *coil* and *loyal* may also be matched. However, the preferred matches are *royal* and *loyal*, and *coil* and *spoil*.

Page 109

Purpose

1. To review words that have the *diphthong* sound of **oi** made by two sets of vowels: **oi** as in **noise** and **oy** as in **boy**.

2. To review the two sounds made by the consonant digraph **th**.

Lesson

Listen to your student read the words in Chart 25.

If the student has no difficulty and can quickly say the words, discuss the lesson and have him answer orally before he completes it independently.

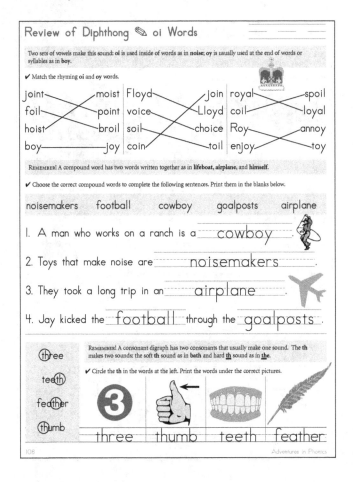

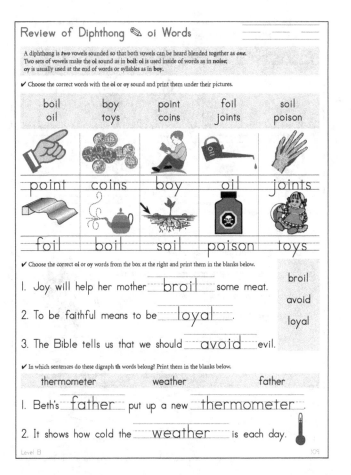

Page 110

Purpose

To review words that have the sound of **är**.

Lesson

Listen to your student read the words in Chart 29 (page 224 in the workbook).

If the student has no difficulty and can quickly say the words, discuss the lesson and have him answer orally before he completes it independently.

Page 111

Purpose

1. To review words that have the sound of **är**.

2. To discuss the importance of suffixes.

Lesson

Listen to your student read the words in Chart 30 (page 224 in the workbook).

If the student has no difficulty and can quickly say the words, discuss the lesson and have him answer orally before he completes it independently.

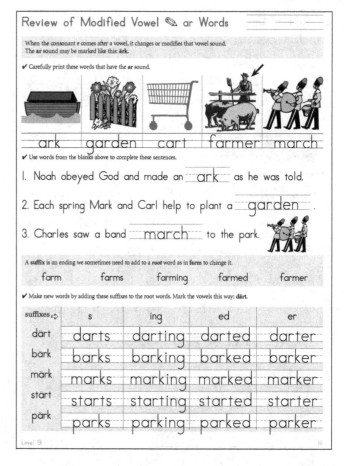

Page 112

Purpose

1. To review words that have the sound of **ôr**.

2. To discuss compound words.

Lesson

Listen to your student read the words in Chart 31 (page 225 in the workbook).

If the student has no difficulty and can quickly say the words, discuss the lesson and have him answer orally before he completes it independently.

Page 113

Purpose

1. To review words that have the sound of **ôr**.

2. To discuss the suffix **ness**.

Lesson

Listen to your student read the words in Chart 31.

If the student has no difficulty and can quickly say the words, discuss the lesson and have him answer orally before he completes it independently.

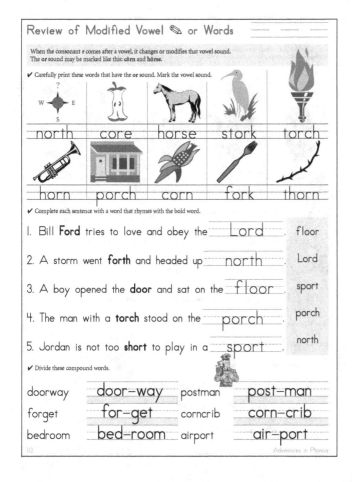

Page 114

Purpose

To review words that have the sound of **ûr** made by **er**, **ir**, and **ur**.

Lesson

Listen to your student read the **er** and **ir** words in Chart 32 and the **ur** words in Chart 33 (page 225 in the workbook).

If the student has no difficulty and can quickly say the words, discuss the lesson and have him answer orally before he completes it independently.

Page 115

Purpose

1. To review words that have the sound of **ûr** made by **ear** and **(w)or**.

2. To review the suffix **er**.

Lesson

Listen as your student reads the words in Chart 33 (page 225 in the workbook) that are spelled with the letters **ear** and **(w)or**.

If the student has no difficulty and can quickly say the words, discuss the lesson and have him answer orally before he completes it independently.

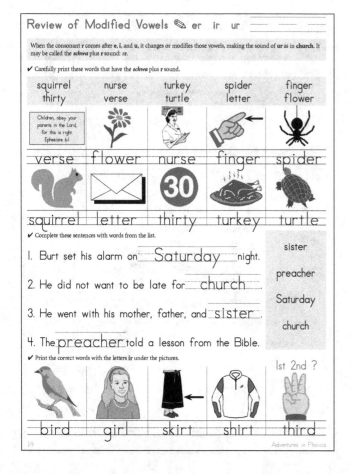

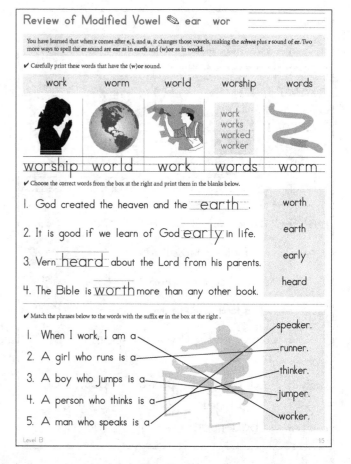

Page 116

Purpose

To review words that have the sound of **âr** as in **are**, **arr**, **air**, **err**, and **ear**.

Lesson

Listen as your student reads the words in Chart 34 (page 226 in the workbook).

If the student has no difficulty and can quickly say the words, discuss the lesson and have him answer orally before he completes it independently.

Page 117

Purpose

To review words that have the sound of **âr** as in **are**, **arr**, **air**, **ear**, **ere**, **err**, and **eir**.

Lesson

If your student can read the words in Chart 34 quickly, you may not feel it necessary to have him read it again.

Discuss the lesson and have your student answer orally before he does the work independently.

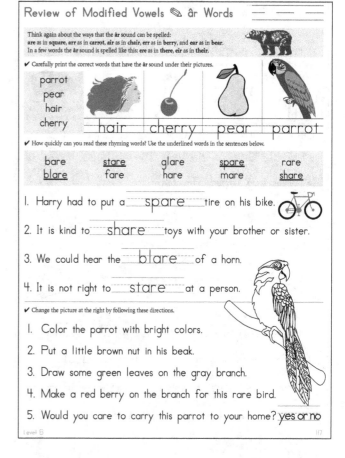

Page 118

Purpose

To review words that have the sound of ô as in d**o**g, b**all**, **au**to, and p**aw**.

Lesson

Listen as your student reads the words in Chart 35 and the first four columns in Chart 36 (page 226 in the workbook).

If the student has no difficulty and can quickly say the words, discuss the lesson and have him answer orally before he completes it independently.

Page 119

Purpose

To review words that have the sound of ô as in d**augh**ter and b**ough**t.

Lesson

Listen as your student reads the last two columns of words in Chart 36.

If the student has no difficulty and can quickly say the words, discuss the lesson and have him answer orally before he completes it independently.

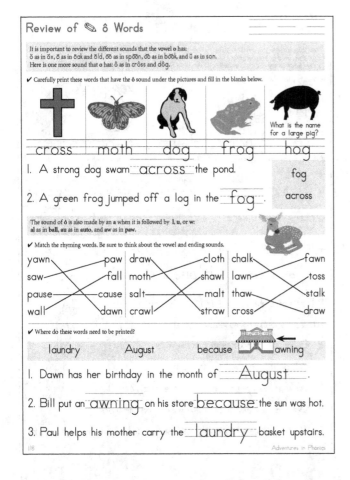

Page 120

Purpose

To review words that have the *soft sound* of **c** as in ice, city, and **cymbals**.

Lesson

Review the rule which teaches that the **c** usually has the sound of **s** when it is followed by the vowels **e, i,** or **y**. The letter **k** makes the hard sound in the words with these vowels, as in **kite, cake,** and **hanky**.

Listen as your student reads the words in Chart 37 (page 227 in the workbook).

If the student has no difficulty and can quickly say the words, discuss the lesson and have him answer orally before he completes it independently.

Page 121

Purpose

To review words that have the *soft sound* of **g** as in **cage, giant,** and **gym**.

Lesson

Review the rule which teaches that the **g** usually has the sound of **j** when it is followed by vowels **e, i,** or **y**. There are a few exceptions such as: **get** and **gift**.

Listen as your student reads the words in Chart 38 (page 227 in the workbook).

If the student has no difficulty and can quickly say the words, discuss the lesson and have him answer orally before he completes it independently.

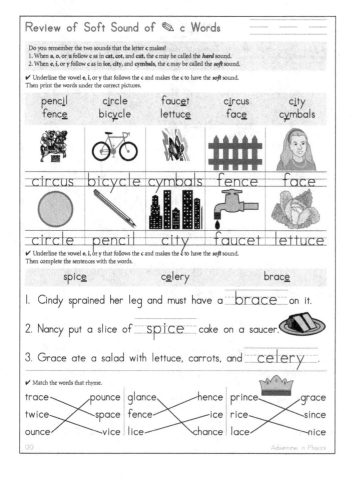

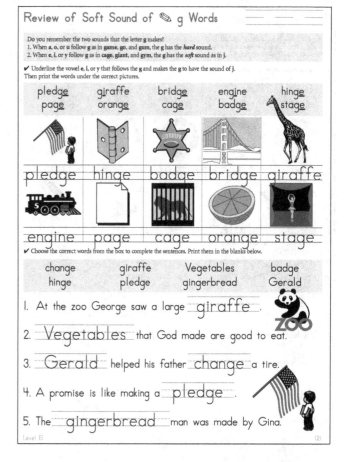

Page 122

Purpose

To review words with the digraphs **sh** and **wh**.

Lesson

Listen as your student reads the **sh** and **wh** words in Charts 8 and 9 (page 217 in the workbook).

If the student has no difficulty and can quickly say the words, discuss the lesson and have him answer orally before he completes it independently.

Page 123

Purpose

To review words with the digraphs **kn** and **wr**.

Lesson

Listen as your student reads the **kn** and **wr** words in Chart 42 (page 228 in the workbook).

If the student has no difficulty and can quickly say the words, discuss the lesson and have him answer orally before he completes it independently.

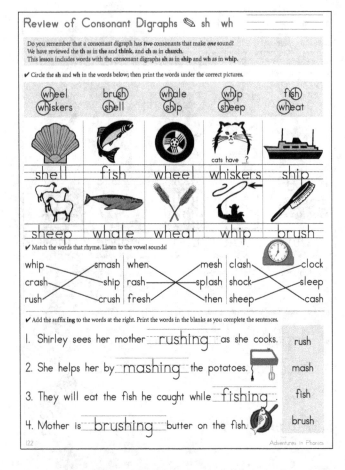

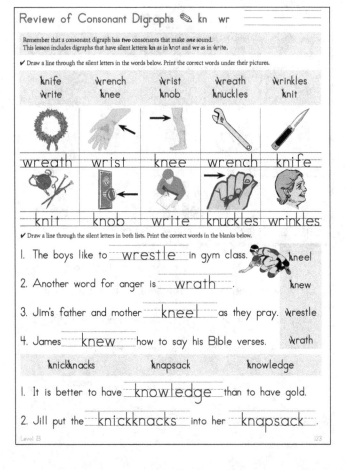

Page 124

Purpose

To review words with silent letters.

Lesson

Carefully and thoroughly discuss the lesson with your student and have him answer orally before he completes it independently.

Page 125

Purpose

To review words with silent letters such as:

calf   walk   watch   calm

It is interesting that the silent letters follow the vowel **a**.

Lesson

Carefully and thoroughly discuss the lesson with your student and have him answer orally before he completes it independently.

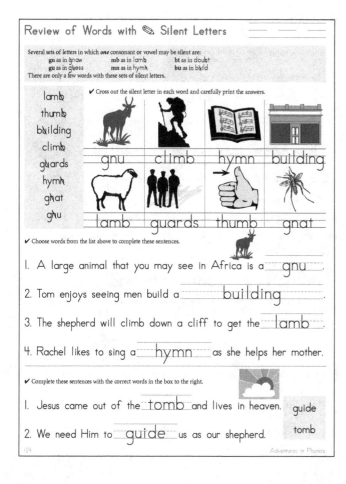

Page 126

Purpose

To review words with the letters **ng** and **nk**.

Lesson

Have your student read these lists of words.

bang	bring	sling	gong
gang	ding	swing	long
hang	fling	spring	wrong
rang	ring	thing	song
sang	sing	wing	thong
bank	rank	ink	rink
blank	sank	blink	sink
crank	tank	drink	think
drank	thank	pink	wink

Listen as your student reads the **ng** and **nk** words in Chart 41 (page 228 in the workbook).

Carefully and thoroughly discuss the lesson and have your student answer orally before he completes it independently.

Page 127

Purpose

To review words with the letters **ea** and **ou**.

Lesson

Chart 40 (page 228 in the workbook) has the three most commonly used words with **ea** having the long sound of **a**. Review the three sounds made by **ea**, and listen as these columns are read by your student.

ĕā	ĕă	ēă
break	bread	ear
steak	thread	heat
great	feather	meal

Have your student read these long **u** words.

you	soup	through
group	wound	youth

Carefully discuss the lesson and have your student answer orally before he completes the work independently.

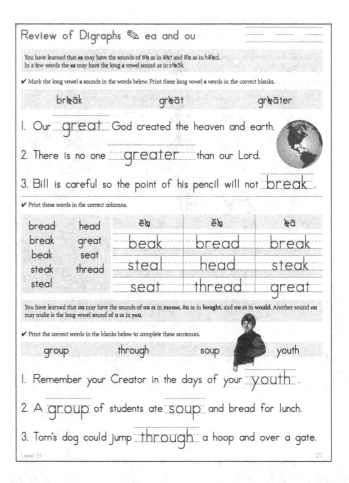

Page 128

Purpose

To work with words that have the vowel **a** making the short sound of **u**. This is called a *schwa* sound and may be made by any of the vowels.

ago   around

Lesson

Carefully discuss the lesson and have your student answer orally before he completes the work independently.

Page 129

Purpose

1. To teach the proper use of **a** and **an** before nouns.

2. Review words with the soft sounds of **c** and **g**.

Lesson

Remind the student about the vowels **a**, **e**, **i**, **o**, and **u**.

Explain that when a word *begins* with a **vowel**, we may use the word **an** before that word as in:

an ant	an apple	an egg
an oar	an owl	an idea
an inch	an eel	an eagle

If a word *begins* with a **consonant**, we would use just the letter **a**, as in:

a book	a car	a piano
a door	a melon	a race

Think about what kind of a letter is at the *beginning* of each word—a **consonant** or a **vowel**.

Discuss the lesson and have your student answer orally before he completes the work independently.

Schwa Sound of ✏ a

Remember that the vowel o may have the short vowel u sound as in these words:

mother   shovel   from   color   wonder   love   Monday   nothing   of

Each of the vowels may make the short sound of u. A dictionary may show a symbol like this ∂ for that sound, which is called a *schwa* sound. Some words begin with the letter a having this sound as in **arose**.

✔ Read these words and then divide them as you print them.

alike	a–like	ago	a–go	alive	a–live
awake	a–wake	asleep	a–sleep	awhile	a–while
afraid	a–fraid	about	a–bout	ahead	a–head
away	a–way	avoid	a–void	astray	a–stray
apart	a–part	arose	a–rose	aloud	a–loud

✔ Use the underlined words above to complete these sentences. Print them in the blanks below.

1. Long **ago** Jesus died on the cross for our sins.

2. Jesus **arose** from the tomb and is **alive** in heaven.

3. He tells us to trust in Him and not to be **afraid**.

4. The Bible tells us **about** many wonderful lessons.

✔ Divide these compound words.

treetop	tree–top	sailboats	sail–boats
milkweed	milk–weed	hillside	hill–side
playmate	play–mate	airway	air–way

128   Adventures in Phonics

Using ✏ a and an

When one object is mentioned, the word an or a may be used when talking about that object.
1. The word a is used before a word that begins with a **consonant**: a car, a doll, or a tack.
2. The word an is used before a word that begins with a **vowel**: an ark, an egg, or an inch.

✔ Notice the beginning letter of each word and think of the rules above about a and **an**.

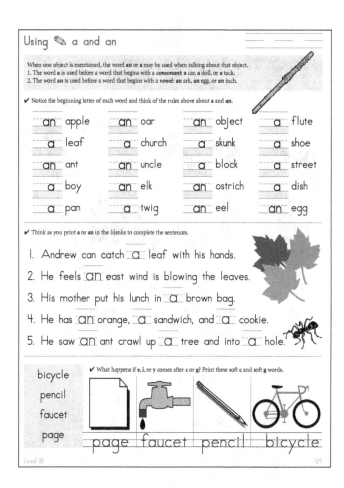

an	apple	an	oar	an	object	a	flute
a	leaf	a	church	a	skunk	a	shoe
an	ant	an	uncle	a	block	a	street
a	boy	an	elk	an	ostrich	a	dish
a	pan	a	twig	an	eel	an	egg

✔ Think as you print a or **an** in the blanks to complete the sentences.

1. Andrew can catch **a** leaf with his hands.

2. He feels **an** east wind is blowing the leaves.

3. His mother put his lunch in **a** brown bag.

4. He has **an** orange, **a** sandwich, and **a** cookie.

5. He saw **an** ant crawl up **a** tree and into **a** hole.

✔ What happens if e, i, or y comes after c or g? Print these soft c and soft g words.

bicycle
pencil
faucet
page

page   faucet   pencil   bicycle

Level B   129

Page 130

Purpose

1. To consider the letter **y** as a *vowel* when it comes at the end of words.

2. To learn that the **y** becomes a *suffix* when added to certain words as in **windy** and **chilly**.

Lesson

Carefully discuss with your student the rules about the vowel "y," as well as the lesson, and have him answer orally before he completes it independently.

Page 131

Purpose

To review the lesson about the letter **y** being a *vowel* when it comes at the end of words.

Lesson

With your student, go over the rules about the vowel "y," as well as the lesson, and have him answer orally before he completes it independently.

---

* Note that with respect to sentences 4 and 5 at the bottom of page 130, their answers may be switched.

Words Ending With The Vowel ✎ y

1. If the y comes after another vowel, it follows the long vowel rule and the y is silent as in dāy and kēy.
2. If the y is the only vowel in the word, it has a long ī sound as in flȳ.
3. If a word has more than one syllable, the y has the long sound of e as in baby (bābē) and lady (lādē).

✔ These words end with y and have two syllables. Print them where they belong.

| kitty | city | pony | penny | candy |
| bunny | cherry | puppy | lady | carry |

| pony | candy | carry | bunny | puppy |
| lady | kitty | cherry | city | penny |

✔ What numbers are these words?

| fifty | **50** | eighty | **80** | forty | **40** | thirty | **30** |
| twenty | **20** | ninety | **90** | sixty | **60** | seventy | **70** |

✔ The suffix y can be added to many words. Add y to the *root* words and complete the sentences.

1. The cold wind made the air feel **chilly** . | chill
2. Jane went outside and she felt it was **windy** | wind
3. It blew her hair so that it was not **curly** | curl
4. She is happy even on **cloudy** days. | cloud
5. She knows that God makes it sunny or **rainy** | rain

130

Words Ending With The Vowel ✎ y

1. If the y comes after another vowel, it follows the long vowel rule and the y is silent as in dāy and kēy.
2. If the y is the only vowel in the word, it has a long ī sound as in flȳ (flī).
3. If a word has more than one syllable, the y has the long sound of e as in baby (bābē) and lady (lādē).

✔ Think of RULES 2 and 3 above as you read these words. Print them in the correct columns.

rocky	sky	chilly	pry	fry
silly	my	why	Mary	needy
try	funny	lady	weary	shy
Sally	windy	cherry	by	happy

y has the long i sound		y has the long e sound	
try	pry	rocky	windy	Mary
sky	by	silly	chilly	weary
my	fry	Sally	lady	needy
why	shy	funny	cherry	happy

✔ Think of RULE 1 as you read these sentences. Print a word in the blanks that is spelled with ay.

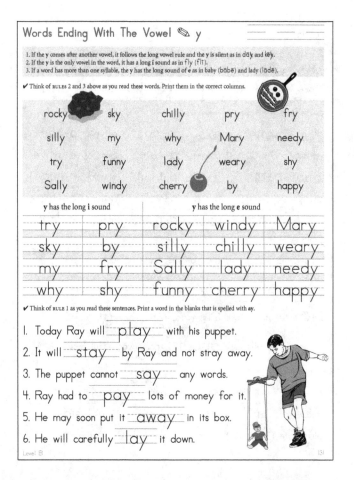

1. Today Ray will **play** with his puppet.
2. It will **stay** by Ray and not stray away.
3. The puppet cannot **say** any words.
4. Ray had to **pay** lots of money for it.
5. He may soon put it **away** in its box.
6. He will carefully **lay** it down.

Level B   131

Page 132

Purpose

To teach the rules about making words ending with **y** *plural.*

Lesson

Thoroughly discuss the rules about making words that end with the vowel **y** *plural* (more than one). Again, the student must know vowels from consonants. If this is the first lesson about plural words, go slowly to help him understand.

Have your student answer orally before he completes the page independently.

Page 133

Purpose

To give additional work in teaching the rules about making words ending with **y** *plural.*

Lesson

Thoroughly discuss the rules about making words that end with the vowel **y** *plural* (more than one). Again, the student must know the difference between vowels and consonants. It is important that your student understands this lesson before he goes on to another page.

Have your student answer orally before he completes the page independently.

Plural Words Ending with ✐ y

An **s** is added to the end of many words when *more than one object* is mentioned (plural) as follows:
cat ➔ cats   book ➔ books   cake ➔ cakes
If a word ends with y, two RULES need to be learned:
1. When the y follows a vowel, just add s as follows: toy ➔ toys, day ➔ days, and key ➔ keys.

✔ Add s to make these words plural. Notice the vowel that comes before the ending y.

valley	valleys	day	days	turkey	turkeys
toy	toys	way	ways	key	keys
joy	joys	tray	trays	boy	boys

The SECOND RULE for words ending with y is:
2. When the y follows a consonant, change the y to i and add es:
city ➔ cities   baby ➔ babies   pony ➔ ponies

✔ Notice the consonant just before the ending y. Change the y to i and add **es** to these words.

lady	ladies	pony	ponies	puppy	puppies
copy	copies	lily	lilies	city	cities
story	stories	bunny	bunnies	duty	duties
penny	pennies	party	parties	candy	candies
fly	flies	worry	worries	kitty	kitties

✔ Notice if a vowel or consonant comes just before the ending y. Think of the two rules above.

1. Brad saw two brown   ponies   in the yard.

2. He saw them run and play for three days .

3. He gathered a basket of berries to eat.

4. Brad picked some   lilies   for his mother.

lily
day
berry
pony

132   Adventures in Phonics

Plural Words Ending With ✐ y

An **s** is added to the end of many words when *more than one object* is mentioned (*plural*) as follows:
cat ➔ cats   book ➔ books   cake ➔ cakes
If a word ends with y, two RULES need to be learned:
1. When the y follows a vowel, just add s as follows: toy ➔ toys, day ➔ days, and key ➔ keys.
2. When the y follows a consonant, change the y to i and add es:
city ➔ cities   baby ➔ babies   pony ➔ ponies

✔ What letter comes before y? Think about these RULES as you make the words plural.

penny	pennies	lily	lilies	cherry	cherries
valley	valleys	fly	flies	tray	trays
baby	babies	supply	supplies	berry	berries
toy	toys	donkey	donkeys	key	keys
turkey	turkeys	pony	ponies	lady	ladies
story	stories	boy	boys	daisy	daisies

✔ Now print these words to be singular or mean *only one.*

turkeys	turkey	stories	story	flies	fly
babies	baby	joys	joy	keys	key
bunnies	bunny	ladies	lady	cities	city

✔ Make the words plural to complete the sentences.

1. A nickel is the same as five   pennies .

2. The farmer had six cows and ten   turkeys .

3. Jerry had three pears and six cherries .

turkey
cherry
penny

Level B   133

Page 134

Purpose

To teach the rule about making words that end with **s**, **x**, **z**, **ch**, and **sh** *plural*.

Lesson

Print the following chart on the board or have your student look at this page. Have him say the underlined letters several times. Teach him this rule:

> If a word ends with **s**, **x**, **z**, **ch**, or **sh**, the letters **-es** are added to make that word *plural*.

s	x	z	sh	ch
cross	box	buzz	bush	arch
crosses	boxes	buzzes	bushes	arches
glass	ax	fizz	crash	latch
glasses	axes	fizzes	crashes	latches
miss	tax	waltz	dish	lunch
misses	taxes	waltzes	dishes	lunches

Carefully go over the lesson and have your student answer orally before he completes the work independently.

Page 135

Purpose

To teach about adding suffixes **-ly** and **-er** to root words.

Lesson

Print the suffixes **-ly** and **-er** on the board. As you pronounce them, say that each suffix has a vowel sound: the **-ly** has the consonant **l** and a long **e** sound, and the **-er** has the *schwa* plus **r** sound as it is heard in words such as work**er**, runn**er**, and help**er**.

Print these words on the board. After your student has read them, add the suffix **-ly** to them and have him read the words again.

> quick   poor   glad   soft

Print these words on the board. After they have been read, add the suffix **-er** to them and have the student read the words again.

> quick   soft   fast   work

Refer to the ending letters **-ly** and **-er** as *suffixes*.

Carefully go over the lesson and have your student answer orally before he completes the work independently.

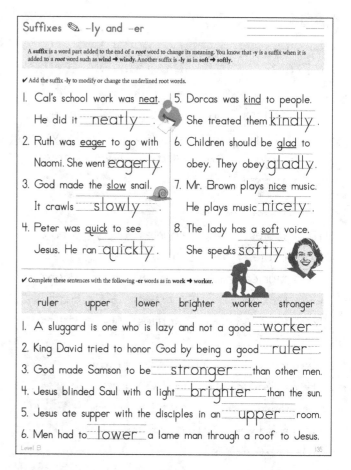

Page 136

Purpose

1. To teach more about **suffixes**.
2. To introduce the definition of **syllable**.

Lesson

Review the meaning of a **suffix**: letters added to the end of a root word to change its meaning.

A **syllable** is a word or part of a word with a vowel sound that is pronounced with a single sound.

Print these words on the board and say them to your student. Clap for each *syllable*:

sis•ter   sum•mer   sil•ver

Each part or *syllable* of these words has a vowel sound. Pronounce and clap the names of other objects that are in your room:

ta•ble   pup•py   moth•er

ba•by   pen•cil   fa•ther

win•dow   cov•er   doc•tor

Carefully go over the lesson and have your student answer orally before he completes the work independently.

Page 137

Purpose

To teach about the suffix **-ful**.

Lesson

Introduce the suffix **-ful** and mention that it has a vowel sound. This means that it is also a *syllable* when it is at the end of a word.

This is an easy lesson, but carefully go over it and have the student answer orally before he does the work by himself.

Suffixes and Syllables ✎ er, or, and ar

Suffixes are letters added to the ends of *root* words to change their meanings as in work ➜ worker.
A **syllable** is a word or part of a word with a vowel sound, which is pronounced with a single sound.

cab ➜ cabin   rob ➜ robin   win ➜ winter   late ➜ later

✔ Complete these sentences with the following -er words. The **er** is part of the last syllable in each word.

answer   brother   bitter   silver   winter

1. Thad's little __brother__ found a __silver__ coin.
2. We should speak kindly when we give an __answer__.
3. The weather had __bitter__ winds during this __winter__.

✔ These words end with **or** and **ar**, which make the *ôr* or *schwa* plus r sound.
Complete the following sentences with **or** and **ar** words in the box. Print them in the blanks below.

doctor   tailor   caterpillar   cellar
beggar   dollar   binoculars   anchor

1. When our neighbor got sick we called a __doctor__.
2. Jesus healed the __beggar__ who had been born blind.
3. Bill had a __tailor__ fix the collar on his suit.
4. Jill found a __caterpillar__ with pretty colors.

✔ Drop the **s** or **es** and add **or** to modify these words. The One who <u>creates</u> is the <u>Creator</u>.

1. One who <u>instructs</u> is an __instructor__
2. One who <u>collects</u> is a __collector__
3. One who <u>directs</u> is a __director__
4. One who <u>operates</u> is an __operator__

Suffix ✎ -ful

REMEMBER: Suffixes are letters added to the ends of words to change their meanings.
The suffix **-ful** means *full of*. The **u** makes a vowel sound, so **-ful** is a syllable.

✔ Carefully add the suffix -ful and read your new words.

peace	peaceful	fear	fearful	shame	shameful
use	useful	care	careful	need	needful
hope	hopeful	skill	skillful	rest	restful
watch	watchful	truth	truthful	pain	painful

✔ Print these words where they belong to complete the sentences.

helpful   faithful   powerful   playful   careful

1. The little brown puppy was __playful__.
2. Tara tries to be __helpful__ to her mother.
3. We should be __careful__ as we print.
4. God is always __faithful__ to His people.
5. He is all __powerful__; with Him nothing is impossible.

A good neighbor is
helpful
thoughtful
thankful
useful
careful
truthful
faithful

✔ Match the phrases in the left-hand columns with the correct -ful words in the right-hand columns.

He who tells the truth is ⟍ restful.   One who thanks is ⟍ careful.
One who is resting is ⟍ truthful.   One who takes care is ⟍ cheerful.
One who helps is ⟍ fearful.   One who has cheer is ⟍ thankful.
Someone who fears is ⟍ helpful.   A sore that has pain is — painful.

Page 138

Purpose

To teach about the suffixes **-less** and **-ness**.

Lesson

Introduce the suffixes **-less** and **-ness** and mention that they each have a vowel sound—the short vowel sound of **e**. This means that they are *syllables* when they are at the end of words.

Carefully go over the lesson and listen to the student answer orally before he does the work by himself.

Page 139

Purpose

To teach the meaning the suffixes **-er** and **-est** have when added to words.

Lesson

Introduce the suffixes **-er** and **-est** and mention that they also have the short vowel sound of **e** and are *syllables*. Explain the meanings they have by printing these words on the board.

root	er	est
soft	softer	softest
hard	harder	hardest

These suffixes help us to tell about differences as we speak.

Bill is **tall**,

Will is **tall<u>er</u>**,

but Phil is **tall<u>est</u>**.

Carefully go over the lesson and listen as your student answers orally before he does the work by himself.

Page 140

Purpose

To teach the three sounds that suffix **-ed** has.

Lesson

Print these columns of words on the board or have your student read from this page. Tell him that **-ed** can say three different sounds. As he reads down the lists, have him listen to the sounds made by the **-ed**.

d	t	ed
called	mixed	rested
climbed	jumped	hunted
sailed	hiked	treated
peeled	thanked	folded

Your student may need to go over this again if it was difficult for him. It may help if he claps as he pronounces the words. In the third column, the "**ed**" has the *schwa* sound, which means it is a *syllable*; therefore, the words would need two claps.

Carefully go over the lesson and listen as your student answers orally before he does the work by himself.

Page 141

Purpose

To teach the rule about adding a **suffix** that begins with a vowel to a word with a short vowel.

Lesson

As you teach the rule written on the top of the page, print these words on the board or have your student look at this page.

If a one-syllable word with a short vowel ends with *one* consonant, *double* that consonant before adding a suffix that begins with a vowel.

root	ed	ing
hop	hopped	hopping
step	stepped	stepping
drip	dripped	dripping
rub	rubbed	rubbing

Ask your student to tell you how many consonants are at the end of the words in the first column above.

Ask: "Does the last letter of each short vowel word below need to be doubled?"

jump   stamp   land   spill

Answer: "No! They end with two consonants."

Sounds of Suffix ✎ -ed

The suffix -ed can make three different sounds:
d as in **cheered** and **called**; t as in **fixed** and **worked**; and ə̄d as in **printed** and **handed**.

PRINT

Conrad call<u>ed</u> his father.   The man work<u>ed</u> hard.   Tom print<u>ed</u> neatly.

✔ As you read these words, underline the -ed sound. Print the sound -ed makes in the blanks: d, t, or ed.

turn<u>ed</u>	d	squirt<u>ed</u>	ed	jump<u>ed</u>	t
fix<u>ed</u>	t	finish<u>ed</u>	t	climb<u>ed</u>	d
hand<u>ed</u>	ed	ask<u>ed</u>	t	hunt<u>ed</u>	ed
serv<u>ed</u>	d	scold<u>ed</u>	ed	push<u>ed</u>	t
rush<u>ed</u>	t	weed<u>ed</u>	ed	groan<u>ed</u>	d

Every syllable has a vowel sound. When the -ed sounds like ə̄d, it makes another syllable as in **handed**.

✔ Listen to the suffix -ed and print how many syllables each word has.

pulled	1	searched	1	called	1
handed	2	carted	2	folded	2
thanked	1	finished	2	greeted	2
cheered	1	walked	1	burned	1

✔ Circle the numeral for the sentences that may be true.

1. Jeff and his sister do not like to read.
②. He is reading a book on plants.
3. A horse is reading a big book about hay.
④. Renee is reading about pretty flowers.

140   Adventures in Phonics

✎ Adding Suffixes

If a one-syllable word with a short vowel ends with *one* consonant, *double* the consonant before adding a suffix that begins with a vowel: hop ➔ hopped ➔ hopper ➔ hopping ➔ hoppy.

✔ Remember to double the ending consonant as you add these suffixes to the short vowel words.

	-ed	-ing		-er	-est
nap	napped	napping	hot	hotter	hottest
shop	shopped	shopping	mad	madder	maddest
rub	rubbed	rubbing	big	bigger	biggest
drip	dripped	dripping	thin	thinner	thinnest
scrub	scrubbed	scrubbing	fat	fatter	fattest
step	stepped	stepping	dim	dimmer	dimmest
tap	tapped	tapping	wet	wetter	wettest

✔ Read the rule again before you add suffixes to these short vowel words. REMEMBER: y may be a vowel.

swim + ing =	swimming	stick + y =	sticky
scrub + er =	scrubber	fog + y =	foggy
jump + ing =	jumping	stiff + est =	stiffest
shag + y =	shaggy	pick + ing =	picking
flat + er =	flatter	stamp + ed =	stamped
trim + ing =	trimming	win + er =	winner
fill + ed =	filled	drip + ing =	dripping

Level B   141

Page 142

Purpose

To teach about **suffixes** and words that end with **e**.

Lesson

Review the rule you studied in the last lesson:

> If a one-syllable word with a short vowel ends with **one** consonant, double that consonant before adding a suffix that begins with a vowel.

<u>rubbed</u>   <u>tapped</u>   <u>hopped</u>   <u>tipped</u>

This lesson has another important rule:

> When a word ends with a silent **e**, drop the **e** before adding a suffix that *begins* with a **vowel**.

root	*ed*	*ing*
joke	joked	joking
close	closed	closing
hope	hoped	hoping
smile	smiled	smiling

When your student understands this rule, carefully go over the lesson and listen as he answers orally before he does the work by himself.

Page 143

Purpose

To review the suffix rules of the past two lessons.

Lesson

Review these rules:

If a one-syllable word with a short vowel ends with one consonant, double that consonant before adding a suffix that begins with a vowel.

fat	big	hit	sun
<u>fat</u>ter	<u>big</u>gest	<u>hit</u>ting	<u>sun</u>ny

These words are divided into *syllables* between the double consonants if the suffix has a vowel sound.

fat-ter	big-gest	hit-ting	sun-ny

When a word ends with a silent **e**, drop the **e** before adding a suffix that *begins* with a **vowel**.

hide	wave	late	drive
hiding	waved	latest	driver

When your student understands these rules, carefully go over the lesson and listen as he answers orally before he does the work by himself.

Suffixes and Words Ending with ✎ e

When a word ends with a silent e, drop the e before adding a suffix that begins with a vowel:
skate ➜ skating, use ➜ used, bake ➜ baker, cute ➜ cutest, shine ➜ shiny.

✔ Add these suffixes to the words ending with a silent e.

	-ed	–ing		-er	-est
wave	waved	waving	tame	tamer	tamest
hope	hoped	hoping	late	later	latest
scrape	scraped	scraping	cute	cuter	cutest
sneeze	sneezed	sneezing	fine	finer	finest
paste	pasted	pasting	ripe	riper	ripest
smile	smiled	smiling	close	closer	closest

✔ Add the suffixes -ed, -er, -est, or -ing to these words as you complete the sentences.

1. Miss White ___invited___ the class to her home.   invite
2. The boys are ___raising___ their hands to answer.   raise
3. I think that Chris is the best ___writer___ in school.   write
4. Tom is always ___joking___ with his father.   joke
5. Mr. Hill's dog had the ___cutest___ puppies.   cute
6. Jim's home is the ___closest___ to church.   close

✔ Underline the suffixes and print the *root* word.

| rais<u>ed</u> | raise | skat<u>er</u> | skate | smil<u>ing</u> | smile |
| fin<u>est</u> | fine | bony | bone | shiny | shine |

142   Adventures in Phonics

✎ Review of Suffixes

When adding a suffix beginning with a <u>vowel</u> (-ed, -er, -ing, -est, or -y) remember two rules:
1. If a one-syllable word with a <u>short vowel</u> ends with a <u>short vowel</u>, **double** that consonant before adding a suffix:
nap ➜ napped, tap ➜ tapping, fat ➜ fattest, wet ➜ wetter, and mud ➜ muddy.
2. If a word ends with a silent e, drop the e before adding a suffix: wave ➜ waving and late ➜ later.

✔ Add the suffixes -er and -est to these short vowel words as you complete the sentences.

1. My cat is <u>fat</u>, Jan's is ___fatter___, but Ted's is ___fattest___.
2. Levi is <u>tall</u>, Ben is ___taller___, but Sam is ___tallest___.
3. Ed's cup is <u>full</u>, Al's is ___fuller___, but mine is ___fullest___.
4. My dog is <u>big</u>, Jill's is ___bigger___, but Kay's is ___biggest___.

✔ Add the suffixes -er and -est to these words that end with e as you complete the sentences.

1. Jon came <u>late</u>, Will came ___later___, but Todd came ___latest___.
2. The pear is <u>ripe</u>, the apple is ___riper___, but the plum is ___ripest___.
3. Our bird is <u>tame</u>, our cat is ___tamer___, but our dog is ___tamest___.
4. Tim lives <u>close</u>, Gail lives ___closer___, but Don lives ___closest___.
5. Dirt is <u>fine</u>, sand is ___finer___, but flour is ___finest___.

✔ Add the suffix -y, which is a vowel, to these words. REMEMBER the rules above.

flop	floppy	drip	drippy
bug	buggy	rose	rosy
sun	sunny	stone	stony
grease	greasy	taste	tasty

Level B   143

Page 144

Purpose

To review the **suffix rules** of the past lessons.

Lesson

Review these rules:

> If a one-syllable word with a short vowel ends with one consonant, double that consonant before adding a suffix that begins with a vowel.

clip	hug	tip	mud
clipper	hugged	tipping	muddy

These words are divided into *syllables* between the double consonants if the suffix has a vowel sound.

clip-per	hugged	tip-ping	mud-dy

> When a word ends with a silent **e**, drop the **e** before adding a suffix that *begins* with a **vowel**.

bake	rose	wise	smile
baker	rosy	wiser	smiled

When your student understands these rules, carefully go over the lesson and listen as he answers orally before he does the work by himself.

Page 145

Purpose

To review the **suffix rules** of the past lessons.

Lesson

Thoroughly review the four rules at the top of the student's page. Suggest that he look at the root words to help him decide how to add the suffixes.

When you think that your student understands these rules, carefully go over the lesson and listen as he answers orally before he does the work by himself.

As is suggested for all of the lessons, correct his work the same day it is completed, talk about any errors, and have them corrected right away.

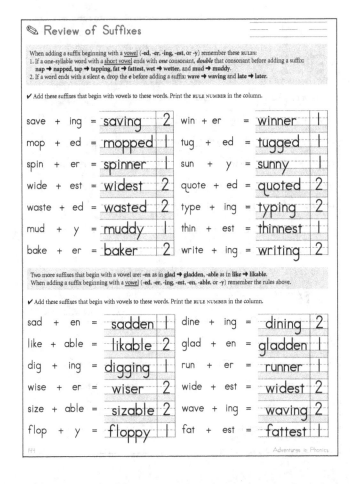

Page 146

Purpose

To review the three rules about adding **suffixes** to words ending with **y**.

Lesson

Review the rules one at a time on the top of the worksheet. Look at each section that matches that rule and use the words for examples. The words in each section match the rule, so the student will not have to decide which rule to apply. However, applying the rule to each word orally should strengthen his understanding.

When your student has a strong understanding of the rules, have him print the answers.

Page 147

Purpose

To review the three rules about adding **suffixes** to words ending with **y**.

Lesson

Repeat your lesson of reviewing the rules one at a time on the top of the worksheet. Looking back at each section on the previous page may be helpful for examples. The words in the top section are varied, so the student will have to think about the rule to apply to the *root* word.

When your student has a good understanding of the rules and has given the answers orally, have him complete the lesson in pencil.

Page 148

Purpose

To review the **suffix rules** of the past lessons.

Lesson

Review the rules on this lesson one at a time, using the words in the sections as examples. Help the student to understand that a *suffix* can be divided from the **root** word *if that suffix has a vowel sound*. Notice these words. Some of the words should not be divided. As the words are pronounced, a reader should be able to sense the division.

s	ed	er	ing
jumps	jumped	jumper	jumping
tests	tested	tester	testing
hauls	hauled	hauler	hauling

Explain that the sounds for the suffix **-ed** sometimes have a vowel sound, and sometimes they do not. For example, the word *jumped* ends with a **t** sound, so it is not divided; but the word *tested* ends with an **ed** sound, so it is divided between the root word and the suffix (test-ed). Ask the student to explain if the word *hauled* would be divided.

When the lesson has been answered orally, have the student complete it independently.

Page 149

Purpose

1. To review the **suffix rules** of the past lessons.
2. To divide compound words.

Lesson

Review this rule:

> A *suffix* is a syllable in itself if it has a vowel sound.

eat-ing	sleep-y	soft-est	knock-er

Explain that each of the words above is divided because *each suffix has a vowel sound*.

Review this rule:

> A *suffix* should not be divided from the root word if the suffix does not have a vowel sound.

desks	shopped	thinks	smiled

Explain that the words *shopped* and *smiled* are not divided because their suffixes do not have a vowel sound. The word *shopped* ends with a **t** sound, and the word *smiled* ends with a **d** sound.

When the lesson has been answered orally, have the student complete it independently.

✏ Review of Words with Suffixes

A **suffix** is a syllable in itself if it has a <u>vowel sound</u> as in **fly-ing, bone-less, land-ed,** and **lunch-es.**

✔ Divide these words into syllables. Do you hear the vowel sound that is in each of these suffixes?

praying	pray-ing	kindness	kind-ness
newest	new-est	speaker	speak-er
helpful	help-ful	painting	paint-ing
sadly	sad-ly	thoughtful	thought-ful
slower	slow-er	softest	soft-est
harmless	harm-less	darkness	dark-ness
tested	test-ed	wisely	wise-ly

A **suffix** is a syllable in itself if it has a <u>vowel sound</u> as in **fly-ing, bone-less, land-ed,** and **lunch-es.** Never divide a combination of letters that are pronounced as one syllable as in **jumped** or **looks.**

✔ Divide these words into syllables. Watch for words with suffixes that should not be divided.

treated	treat-ed	helper	help-er
feared	feared	smallest	small-est
reading	read-ing	trusted	trust-ed
careful	care-ful	greedy	greed-y
works	works	called	called

✔ Underline the words in these verses that have suffixes.

- <u>Blessed</u> is the man who always <u>fears</u> the Lord. (Proverbs 28:14a)
- Make a <u>joyful</u> noise unto God. (Psalm 66:1a)

148   Adventures in Phonics

✏ Review of Words with Suffixes

A **suffix** is a syllable in itself if it has a <u>vowel sound</u> as in **fly-ing, bone-less, land-ed,** and **lunch-es.**

✔ Each of the sentences has **two** words with **suffixes**. Underline the words and divide them as you print them. Watch for words with suffixes that should not be divided.

	1 Syllable Words	2 Syllable Words
1. Chuck <u>wants</u> to be <u>helpful</u> to dad.	wants	help-ful
2. He <u>thinks</u> about the Bible <u>teaching</u>.	thinks	teach-ing
3. He is <u>blessed</u> when he is <u>praying</u>.	blessed	pray-ing
4. They will be <u>watching</u> his good <u>works</u>.	works	watch-ing
5. You will be <u>thinking</u> about her <u>deeds</u>.	deeds	think-ing
6. He <u>knows</u> a <u>lying</u> word will hurt them.	knows	ly-ing

REMEMBER! If a word ends with **s, x, z, ch,** or **sh,** add **es** to make it plural:
bus ➔ buses, box ➔ boxes, buzz ➔ buzzes, lunch ➔ lunches, and **dish ➔ dishes.**

✔ The **e** makes a vowel sound that makes **es** to be a syllable. Divide these words.

catches	catch-es	marches	march-es
mixes	mix-es	taxes	tax-es
dishes	dish-es	dresses	dress-es
reaches	reach-es	buzzes	buzz-es

✔ Divide these compound words.

footprints	foot-prints	stairway	stair-way
highway	high-way	popcorn	pop-corn
tonight	to-night	necktie	neck-tie

Level B   149

Page 150

Purpose

1. To teach about the prefixes **un-** and **dis-**.
2. To work with words with *opposite* meanings.

Lesson

Explain the **prefix rule** at the top of the lesson, using the words in that section for examples.

When your student has a good understanding of the page and has given the answers orally, have him complete the lesson in pencil.

Page 151

Purpose

To teach about the prefixes **re-**, **de-**, and **pre-**.

Lesson

Discuss the definition of a *prefix* as it is explained in the rule at the top of the lesson, using the words in that section for examples.

When your student has given the answers orally and has a good understanding of the page, have him complete the lesson in pencil.

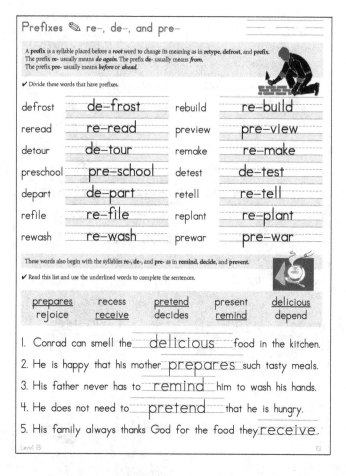

Page 152

Purpose

To teach about the prefixes **ex-**, **fore-**, and **for-**.

Lesson

Discuss the definitions of prefixes **ex-**, **fore-**, and **for-** as explained in the rules at the top of the lesson.

When your student has given the answers orally and has a good understanding of the page, have him complete the lesson in pencil.

Page 153

Purpose

To teach about the prefix **be-**.

Lesson

Introduce the prefix **be-**, using the words in the exercise box for examples.

When your student has given the answers orally and has a good understanding of the page, have him complete the lesson in pencil.

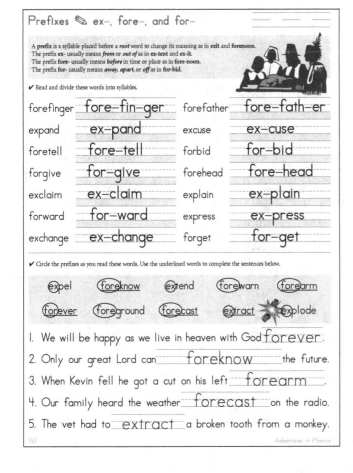

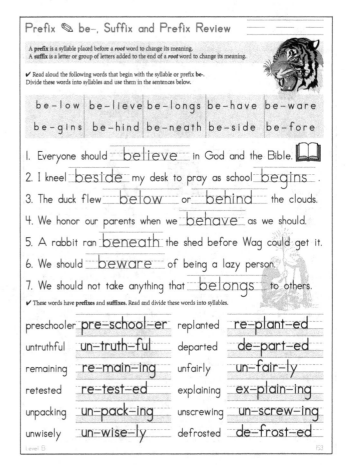

Page 154

Purpose

To teach the rules regarding one-syllable words and compound words.

Lesson

Review the definition of a *syllable*.

> A *syllable* is a word or part of a word with one vowel sound and is pronounced with a single sound of the voice.

> hand   door   tree   straight

Because these words have only one vowel sound, **Rule One** states:

> A one-syllable word must never be divided.

Since compound words are made up of two or more words, **Rule Two** says:

> Divide a compound word between the words that make the compound word.

> grape–vine   moon-light

> some–where   in–to

When your student understands these rules, carefully go over the lesson and listen as he reads the words orally before he does the work by himself.

Page 155

Purpose

To teach the rules about dividing words that have a **suffix** or **prefix**.

Lesson

Review about each syllable having one vowel sound as in **catch**, **smart**, **know**, **swing**, etc.

Talk about words having a suffix such as:

> faith–ful   laugh–ing   hope–less

Discuss **Rule Three** about suffixes:

> When a word has a suffix that makes a vowel sound, divide the word between the root word and the suffix.

Talk about words having a prefix such as:

> un–lock   dis–please   fore–arm

Discuss **Rule Four** about prefixes:

> When a word has a prefix that makes a vowel sound, divide the word between the prefix and the root word.

When your student understands these rules, carefully go over the lesson and listen as he reads the words orally before he does the work by himself.

✎ Rules One and Two for Dividing Words

Rule One: A one-syllable word must never be divided.

✔ Try to print these one-syllable words without looking at the list. They should never be divided.

deer	cross	clock	mouse	square
heart	wrench	check	goose	write

clock   write   heart   cross   goose

mouse   deer   square   check   wrench

Rule Two: Divide a compound word between the words that make the compound word.

✔ Divide these compound words. Try to print the names of the pictures without looking at the list.

foot–ball	wind–mill	home–work	barn–yard
hair–cut	tip–toe	base–ball	blue–bird
snow–flake	stair–way	work–man	clip–board
sail–boat	side–walk	out–let	fish–bowl

bluebird   clipboard   sailboat   windmill

workman   baseball   stairway   fishbowl

154   Adventures in Phonics

✎ Rules Three and Four for Dividing Words

Rule Three: When a word has a suffix that makes a vowel sound, divide the word between the *root* word and the **suffix**.

✔ Divide these words with suffixes. See how quickly you can read them.

thoughtful	thought–ful	throwing	throw–ing
parting	part–ing	helper	help–er
kindness	kind–ness	careless	care–less
wisely	wise–ly	thinking	think–ing
joyful	joy–ful	faithful	faith–ful
jumping	jump–ing	highest	high–est
smallest	small–est	sweetness	sweet–ness

Rule Four: When a word has a prefix that makes a vowel sound, divide the word between the **prefix** and the *root* word.

✔ Divide these words with prefixes. See how quickly you can read them.

unsafe	un–safe	explode	ex–plode
displease	dis–please	depart	de–part
derail	de–rail	unchain	un–chain
rebuild	re–build	explore	ex–plore
forenoon	fore–noon	around	a–round
prepaid	pre–paid	forehead	fore–head
beside	be–side	preview	pre–view

Level B   155

Page 156

Purpose

To review prefixes **un-**, **dis-**, **ex-**, and **re-**.

Lesson

Carefully go over the rules and directions in the lesson. In addition, simply explain that some words have three syllables, as in **dis-o-bey** and **ex-cit-ed**.

Note that the rule for dividing words like **obey** is first stated on page 183 of the workbook; therefore, do not stress this presently. The important concept here is dividing words after prefixes.

When your student understands these rules, listen as he reads the words orally before he does the work by himself.

Page 157

Purpose

1. To review prefixes **pre-**, **fore-**, and **for-**.
2. To teach the prefix **in-**.

Lesson

Carefully go over the rules and directions in the lesson.

When your student understands these rules, listen as he reads the words orally before he does the work by himself.

Remind your student that the letter **a** may take the *schwa* sound, especially at the beginning of a word.

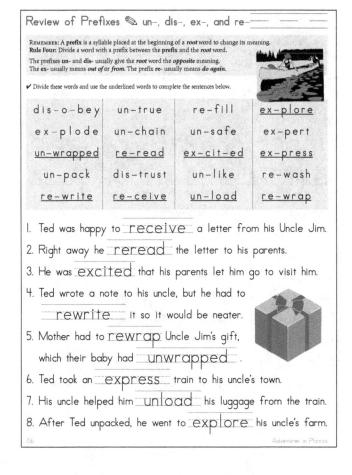

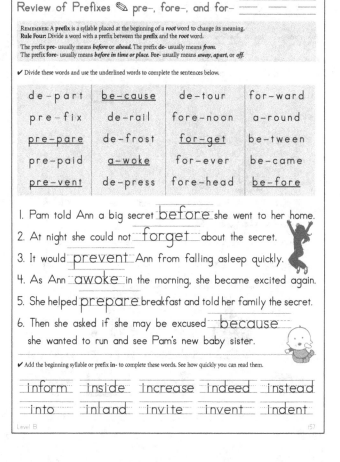

Page 158

Purpose

To teach about *accents* in words.

Lesson

Spend enough time on this lesson to help your student understand about accents.

Say these words correctly, then incorrectly.

mar′ble	*not*	mar ble′
help′ful	*not*	help ful′
cloud′y	*not*	cloud y′
re turn′	*not*	re′turn

Carefully go over the rules and directions in the lesson.

When your student understands these rules, listen as he reads the words orally before he does the work by himself.

Note the word **refill** in the list of words at the top of page 158 may also have the accent on the first syllable if it is a noun.

Page 159

Purpose

To teach about the *schwa* sound made by any of the vowels in the **unaccented** syllable of certain words.

Lesson

Say these words to your student, explaining that the **unaccented** syllable (in these words it is the last syllable, except for the two words that begin with the *schwa* sound of **a**) has the short vowel sound which is like the short **u** sound:

Je′s<u>u</u>s	bot′t<u>o</u>m	<u>a</u> go′
cam′<u>e</u>l	man′n<u>a</u>	<u>a</u> round′

Carefully go over the rules and directions in the lesson with your student.

When he has a good understanding, listen as he reads the words orally before he does the work by himself.

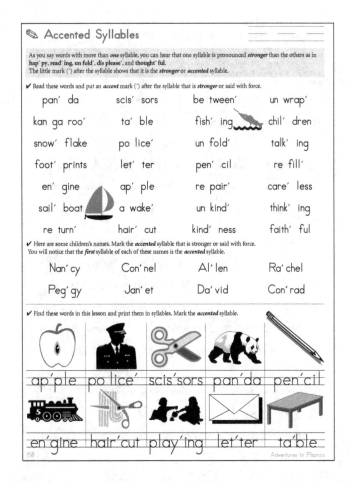

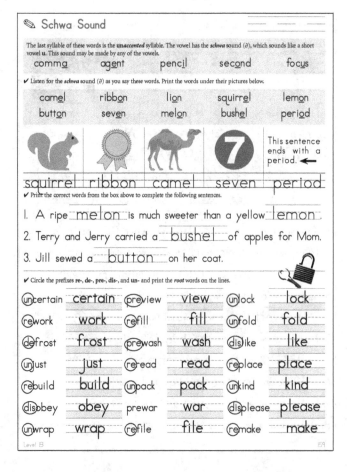

Page 160

Purpose

1. To teach about more words that have the *schwa* sound made by the vowel **a**.

2. To review adding the suffix **y** to short vowel words.

Lesson

Carefully go over the rules and directions in the lesson with your student.

When he has a good understanding, listen as he reads the words orally before he does the work by himself.

Page 161

Purpose

1. To teach about words with the *schwa* sound made by the letters **le**.

2. To teach how words ending with **le** are to be divided.

Lesson

Carefully go over the rules and directions in the lesson with your student.

When he has a good understanding, listen as he reads the words orally before he does the work by himself.

Review of Schwa Sound ✎ a Words

The letter **a** at the beginning of these words is the first syllable. It is the **un**accented syllable and has the *schwa* sound as in **ago, away,** and **around.** A dictionary may show it this way: ∂ **go.**

✔ Read the words and divide them into syllables. The *accent* mark belongs on the second syllable.

afraid	a–fraid′	along	a–long′
ahead	a–head′	alone	a–lone′
again	a–gain′	amount	a–mount′
apart	a–part′	awake	a–wake′
around	a–round′	aside	a–side′
awhile	a–while′	alike	a–like′

✔ Choose words from the list to complete these sentences.

1. Al was __awake__ all day, but then he fell asleep.
2. Mr. Sherman told us __about__ many Bible stories.
3. Jesus __arose__ from the grave after three days.
4. We should obey Him as we __await__ His coming.
5. We should __avoid__ being foolish in all things.
6. The Bible says to stay __away__ from wicked people.

avoid
about
away
awake
await
arose

✔ Double the last consonant and add y to these short vowel words. Divide them into syllables.

mud	mud–dy	pup	pup–py	fog	fog–gy
fun	fun–ny	drip	drip–py	shag	shag–gy
crab	crab–by	snap	snap–py	flop	flop–py

160   Adventures in Phonics

Schwa Sound ✎ le Words

These words have *two* or *three* syllables and end with **le**. The first syllable is *accented*. In the last syllable the **e** has the *schwa* sound as in **ta′ ble, bu′ gle, cat′ tle,** and **puz′ zle.**

people
eagle
bugle
bicycle
apple
triangle
circle
turtle

✔ Carefully print the correct words under the following pictures.

turtle   bicycle   eagle   apple
circle   bugle   triangle   people

✔ Choose le words from the box at the right to complete these sentences. Print them in the blanks below.

1. Ted had pizza and a __bottle__ of juice.
2. After Hannah fed an __apple__ to her pony, she put a __bridle__ and __saddle__ on him.
3. She led him from the __stable__ to ride him.
4. Jenny put a pretty __candle__ on the table for light.
5. It would be nice to visit an old English __castle__.

apple
castle
candle
saddle
bottle
stable
bridle

When words ending with **le** are divided, the consonant just before the **le** is usually part of the last syllable as in **ta′ ble, bu′ gle, cat′ tle,** and **puz′ zle.**

✔ Divide these words into syllables.

gentle	gen–tle	jungle	jun–gle	tumble	tum–ble
dimple	dim–ple	middle	mid–dle	little	lit–tle
riddle	rid–dle	single	sin–gle	purple	pur–ple

Level B   161

Page 162

Purpose

1. To teach more about words with the *schwa* sound made by the letters **le**.

2. To give more practice in dividing words that end with **le**.

Lesson

Carefully go over the rules and directions in the lesson with your student.

When he has a good understanding, listen as he reads the words orally before he does the work by himself.

Schwa Sound ✎ le Words

It is fun to learn about the many words that end with **le**. Here is another lesson with them.

✔ Match the phrases with the pictures. NOTE: The underlined words end with the *schwa* plus l sound of **le**.

1. a <u>little</u> turtle in a <u>puddle</u>
2. a <u>single</u> apple on a <u>table</u>
3. a child with a <u>dimple</u>
4. a <u>needle</u> and a <u>thimble</u>
5. a <u>candle</u> on a <u>table</u>
6. a star with a <u>twinkle</u>
7. a <u>ruffle</u> on a <u>cradle</u>
8. a <u>bundle</u> of <u>purple</u> socks

✔ Print the correct words under the following pictures.

| handle | ankle | middle | bridle | castle |
| saddle | bottle | paddle | needle | bubbles |

bridle   bubbles   paddle   middle   saddle

bottle   needle   handle   ankle   castle

REMEMBER! The consonant just before the **le** is usually part of the last syllable as in **sin´gle** and **ta´ble**.

✔ Divide these words as you say them. Do you notice that the first syllable follows the vowel rules?

| grumble | grum–ble | pebble | peb–ble | sparkle | spar–kle |
| wiggle | wig–gle | bundle | bun–dle | jumble | jum–ble |

162   Adventures in Phonics

Page 163

Purpose

1. To teach about words with the *schwa* sound ending with **ckle**.

2. To teach about dividing words that end with **ckle** or **le**.

Lesson

Print these words on the board/paper or have your student look at this page.

| -b∂l | -d∂l | -b∂l |
| marble | handle | crumble |

Discuss the rule about dividing the word with a consonant staying with the **le**.

Do the same with these words.

| -k∂l | -k∂l | -k∂l |
| pickle | tackle | freckle |

Teach the rule that in words ending with **ckle**, the **le** stands alone. The letters **ck** must always be with the short vowel sound.

Carefully go over the rules and directions in the lesson with your student.

When he has a good understanding, listen as he reads the lists of words orally before he does the work by himself.

Schwa Sound ✎ ckle Words

These words have the consonant digraph **ck** followed by **le** as in **pick´le**. The consonant **ck** must never be divided. The **ck** stays with the short vowel in the first syllable, so the **le** does not have another consonant in the last syllable as in **buck´le**. The **le** stands alone.

✔ Do you see the **ck** in these words? Divide the words right after the **ck** as in **chuck´le**.

| pick–le | crack–le | buck–le | trick–le | shack–le |
| tick–le | chuck–le | tack–le | freck–le | speck–le |

✔ Where do these words belong?

buckle
cradle
rattle
pickle
cattle
freckles
fiddle
puddle

pickle   cattle   rattle   fiddle

cradle   freckles   buckle   puddle

REMEMBER! When a **ck** is in a word, divide the word right after the **ck** as in **tack´le**.
If there is no **ck** in the word, a consonant is usually part of the **le** as in **ta´ble** and **tur´tle**.

✔ Divide these words.

needle	nee–dle	bundle	bun–dle	turtle	tur–tle
prickle	prick–le	sprinkle	sprin–kle	middle	mid–dle
snuggle	snug–gle	jungle	jun–gle	struggle	strug–gle
ripple	rip–ple	speckle	speck–le	rumble	rum–ble
chuckle	chuck–le	cable	ca–ble	fumble	fum–ble
eagle	ea–gle	tackle	tack–le	crackle	crack–le

Level B   163

Page 164

Purpose

1. To review several of the sounds made by the vowel **a**.

2. To have additional practice with **le** words.

Lesson

Print these sounds and words on the board/paper and talk about the sounds of the vowel **a**. Does your student know and hear these sounds of the **a**?

ă	ā	a
hand	pray	along
tag	train	away
saddle	stable	alike
map	gate	around

After discussing each line, have him mark the **a**.

Carefully go over the rules and directions in the lesson with your student.

When he has a good understanding, listen as he gives the answers orally before he does the work by himself.

Page 165

Purpose

1. To review words with the soft **c** or **g** that end with the silent **e**.

2. To teach that some words ending with the sound of **s**, **r**, or **v** may end with a silent **e**.

Lesson

Review the rules about the letters **c** and **g** having the soft sound when followed by **e**, **i**, or **y** as in the following words:

ice	nice	face	grace
pencil	age	cage	edge
edge	ginger	cymbal	gym

Explain that some words ending with the sound made by **s**, **r**, or **v** may end with a silent **e** even if the vowel is not a long vowel sound, such as:

have	give	shove	goose
more	love	care	glove

Carefully go over the rules and directions in the lesson with your student.

When he has a good understanding, listen as he gives the answers orally before he does the work by himself.

Page 166

Purpose

1. To review that the vowels **i** and **o** may sometimes have the long vowel sound even when they are the only vowel in the word.

2. To teach about adding the suffix **-ing** to words ending with **w**, **x**, or **y**.

Lesson

Review the rule that a single **i** usually is short, except when it is followed by **ld**, **nd**, or **gh**. The **gh** is silent.

| child | mild | find | kind | right |

Also review the rule that a single **o** usually has the short sound, but may have the long vowel sound when followed by two consonants such as **ld**, **st**, **th**, **ll**, and **lt**.

| cold | most | both | stoll | colt |

Carefully discuss the rule about adding the suffix **-ing** to words ending with **w**, **x**, or **y**.

| bowing | taxing | crying | playing |

When your student seems to understand the lesson, listen as he gives the answers orally before he does the work by himself.

Page 167

Purpose

1. To review the **ûr** sound made with sets of letters **er**, **ir**, **ur**, **ear**, and **(w)or**.

2. To review the rule about doubling the last consonant of a short vowel word when adding a suffix beginning with a vowel such as **-ing**.

Lesson

Reading the words on Charts 32 and 33 (page 225 in the workbook) would be good drill for reviewing the modified **er** sound.

When your student seems to understand the lesson, listen as he gives the answers orally before he does the work by himself.

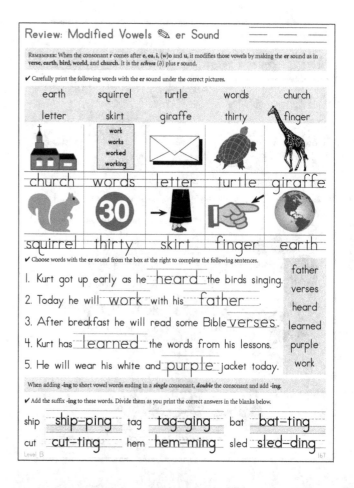

Page 168

Purpose

1. To review the three sounds made by the letters **ear**: **ear** as in **dear**, **ear** as in **earth**, and **ear** as in **pear**.

2. To review the rule about adding **-es** when making words that end with **s**, **x**, **z**, **ch**, or **sh** *plural*.

Lesson

Ask your student to say these sounds and words:

ēₐr	eₐr	ᵌâr
dear	earn	bear
fear	earth	pear
gear	learn	tear
hear	pearl	wear
near	search	swear

Review the rule about adding **-es** to make words that end with **s**, **x**, **z**, **ch**, or **sh** *plural*. (See page 134 in the workbook.)

When the student understands the page and has given the answers orally, have him do the work by himself.

Page 169

Purpose

To review the three sounds made by the vowels **ea**.

Lesson

Ask your student to say these sounds and words:

ēₐ	ᵌā	ĕₐ
deal	break	bread
flea	great	deaf
leap	steak	head
meal	breaking	health
sea	greater	meant

When he understands the page and has given the answers orally, have him do the work by himself.

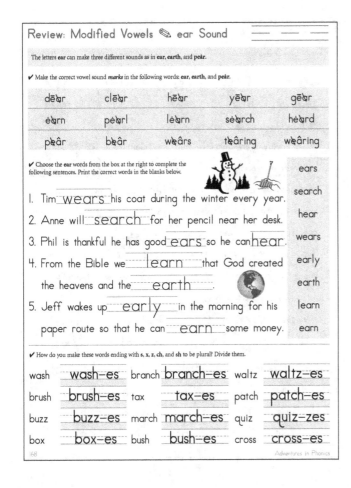

Review: Modified Vowels ✎ ear Sound

The letters **ear** can make three different sounds as in **ear**, **earth**, and **pear**.

✔ Make the correct vowel sound *marks* in the following words: **ear**, **earth**, and **pear**.

dēₐr	clēₐr	hēₐr	yēₐr	gēₐr
eₐrn	peₐrl	leₐrn	seₐrch	heₐrd
peâr	beâr	weârs	teâring	weâring

✔ Choose the **ear** words from the box at the right to complete the following sentences. Print the correct words in the blanks below.

1. Tim __wears__ his coat during the winter every year.
2. Anne will __search__ for her pencil near her desk.
3. Phil is thankful he has good __ears__ so he can __hear__.
4. From the Bible we __learn__ that God created the heavens and the __earth__.
5. Jeff wakes up __early__ in the morning for his paper route so that he can __earn__ some money.

Box: ears, search, hear, wears, early, earth, learn, earn

✔ How do you make these words ending with **s**, **x**, **z**, **ch**, and **sh** to be plural? Divide them.

wash	wash-es	branch	branch-es	waltz	waltz-es
brush	brush-es	tax	tax-es	patch	patch-es
buzz	buzz-es	march	march-es	quiz	quiz-zes
box	box-es	bush	bush-es	cross	cross-es

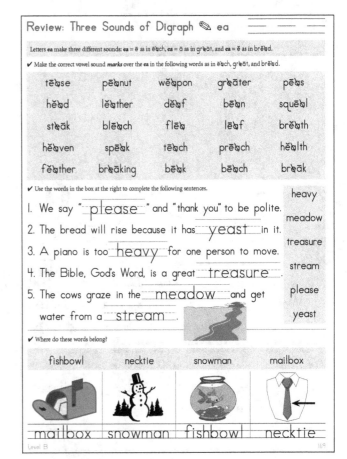

Review: Three Sounds of Digraph ✎ ea

Letters **ea** make three different sounds: **ea** = ē as in **each**, **ea** = ā as in **great**, and **ea** = ĕ as in **bread**.

✔ Make the correct vowel sound *marks* over the ea in the following words as in **each**, **great**, and **bread**.

tēₐse	pēₐnut	wĕₐpon	grēₐter	pēₐs
hĕₐd	lĕₐther	dĕₐf	bēₐn	squēₐl
stēₐk	blēₐch	flēₐ	lēₐf	brĕₐth
hĕₐven	spēₐk	tēₐch	prēₐch	hĕₐlth
fĕₐther	brēₐking	bēₐk	bēₐch	brēₐk

✔ Use the words in the box at the right to complete the following sentences.

1. We say "__please__" and "thank you" to be polite.
2. The bread will rise because it has __yeast__ in it.
3. A piano is too __heavy__ for one person to move.
4. The Bible, God's Word, is a great __treasure__.
5. The cows graze in the __meadow__ and get water from a __stream__.

Box: heavy, meadow, treasure, stream, please, yeast

✔ Where do these words belong?

| fishbowl | necktie | snowman | mailbox |

| __mailbox__ | __snowman__ | __fishbowl__ | __necktie__ |

Page 170

Purpose

To review words ending with the long vowel sound.

Lesson

Talk about the long vowel sound that is made by one vowel at the end of these words:

o	e	i*	y
go	be	hi	cry
lo	he	hi-fi	dry
ho	me	pi	fry
no	she	chi	shy
so	we	Wi-Fi	try

* Note that the long **i** words are not required, but the student should be aware of them. The words *pi* (π) and *chi* (χ) are names for letters from the Greek alphabet and are used in mathematical equations.

Listen as your student reads the long vowel words in Chart 20 (page 221 in the workbook), and discuss the exceptions to the rule.

When your student understands the page and has given the answers orally, have him do the work independently.

Page 171

Purpose

To teach words with **ie** making the long vowel **e** sound.

Lesson

Talk about the vowels **ie** sometimes making the long vowel **e** sound, and ask your student to read these words:

chief	relief	niece
thief	field	shriek
grief	yield	fierce*
brief	shield	pier*
belief	priest	pierce*

* Explain that words with the vowel digraph **ie** followed by the letter **r** make the modified vowel sound of **ear** (ē͝r).

When your student understands the page and has given the answers orally, have him do the work independently.

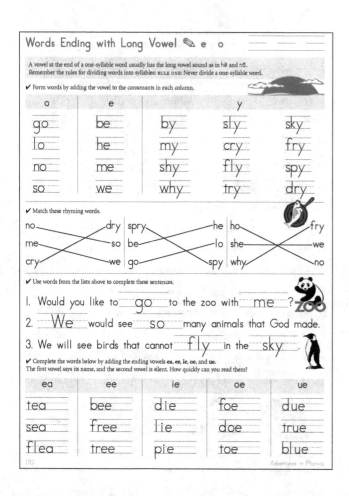

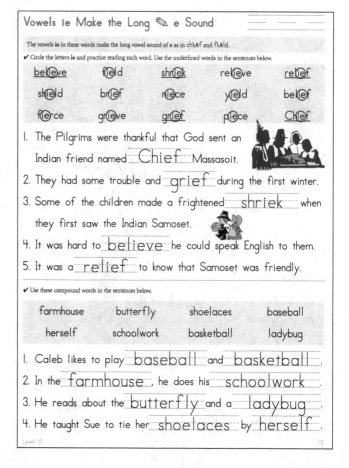

Page 172

Purpose

To review words with the sound of **ô** made by the letters **o** or **al**.

Lesson

It would be a good drill for your student to read the words in the first five columns of Chart 35 (page 226 in the workbook).

When the student understands the page and has given the answers orally, have him do the work independently.

Page 173

Purpose

To review words with the sound of **ô** made by the letters **aw**, **ough**, and **augh**.

Lesson

Listen to your student read the words in Chart 36.

When the student understands the page and has given the answers orally, have him do the work independently.

Review of ô Words

Do you remember the different sounds that the vowel o has?

o as in **ox**   ō as in **ōlεk**   ōō as in **spōōn**   ŏŏ as in **bŏŏk**   ô as in **crôss**   ŭ as in **son**

✔ Match these words with their meanings. Use the underlined words in the following sentences.

1. gloss	3 angry		1. lost	2 frozen dew	
2. toss	2 throw		2. frost	3 the price	
3. cross	4 green plant		3. cost	4 not on	
4. <u>moss</u>	1 shine		4. <u>off</u>	1 not found	

1. <u>log</u>	4 a large pig		1. moth	4 not hard	
2. fog	3 hopping animal		2. broth	1 an insect	
3. <u>frog</u>	2 clouds near land		3. cloth	3 used for clothes	
4. hog	1 part of tree		4. soft	2 thin soup	

1. Al sees a <u>frog</u> on a log that is covered with <u>moss</u>.

2. He will try to catch it before it jumps <u>off</u> the <u>log</u>.

When the vowel **a** is followed by an **l**, it usually has the ô sound as in **hall**, **walk**, and **salt**.

✔ Match these words with their meanings.

1. all	4 little		1. walk	2 a plant stem	
2. halt	3 tumble over		2. stalk	3 a passageway	
3. fall	2 stop		3. hall	4 speak or yell	
4. small	1 everything		4. call	1 move on foot	

172   Adventures in Phonics

Review of ô Words

The sound of ô is often made with the letters aw as in **law** and **claw**.

✔ Match these words with their meanings.

1. jaw	4 chews		1. hawk	4 begins to melt	
2. paw	1 part of mouth		2. dawn	3 grassy yard	
3. straw	2 animal's foot		3. lawn	1 large bird	
4. gnaws	3 dried grain stalk		4. thaws	2 early morning	

1. crawl	4 terrible		1. awning	3 not cooked	
2. claw	3 young deer		2. yawn	4 cutting tool	
3. fawn	2 bird's sharp nail		3. raw	1 cover for shade	
4. awful	1 move like baby		4. saw	2 deep breath	

The sound of ô may also be spelled with the letters **ough** as in **bought** and **augh** as in **caught**.

✔ Print these words next to their meanings. Use the underlined words in the sentences below.

taught   caught   <u>daughter</u>   brought   <u>thought</u>   naughty   <u>bought</u>   <u>ought</u>

did teach	taught		did think	thought
a parents' girl	daughter		to not behave	naughty
did catch	caught		did buy	bought
did bring	brought		should	ought

1. Mrs. Smith <u>bought</u> a toy bear for her <u>daughter</u>.

2. Anne <u>thought</u> that it was tired and <u>ought</u> to sleep.

Level B   173

Page 174

Purpose

To review words with the sound of **ô** made with the letters **ough** or **augh**.

Lesson

Can your student quickly read the words in the last two columns of Chart 36 (page 226 in the workbook)? If not, it would be good to have him read them several times.

When he understands the page and has given the answers orally, have him do the work independently.

Page 175

Purpose

To review more words with the sound of **ô** made by **al** and **aw**.

Lesson

Can your student quickly read the words in the fourth and fifth columns of Chart 35, and the first four columns of Chart 36? If not, have him read them several times.

When he understands the page and has given the answers orally, have him do the work independently.

Page 176

Purpose

1. To review words with the long **u** vowel sound made with the letters **ew**.

2. To review the rule about adding **-es** when making words that end with **s, x, z, ch**, or **sh** *plural*.

Lesson

Listen to your student read the words in the last three columns of Chart 19 (page 221 in the workbook).

When he understands the page and has given the answers orally, have him do the work independently.

Page 177

Purpose

1. To review **âr** words made with the letters **air**.

2. To review rules about dividing short vowel words having the suffix **-ing**.

Lesson

Ask your student to read these words:

air   pair   hair   fair   stair

Carefully review this rule:

When a **short vowel word** ends with a single consonant, that consonant is usually doubled before adding a suffix that begins with a vowel.

hop ⇒ hop|ping   win ⇒ win|ning

These words should be divided right after the root word, which is between the double letters.

You know that many short vowel words end with the double letters: **ff, ll, ss**, and **zz**.

These words should be divided after those double letters.

puff|ing   fill|ing   miss|ing   buzz|ing

After answering orally, your student should be ready to do the work by himself.

Review Lesson of ✏ ew Words

Words ending with the long vowel **u** sound often end with the spelling **ew**. The *w* is used as a vowel.

✔ Match these words with their meanings. Use the underlined words to complete the sentences below.

drew	knew	threw	flew	hew	pew	brew
crew	grew	blew	chew	new	stew	dew

group of workers	crew	thick soup	stew
did draw	drew	water on lawn	dew
eat with teeth	chew	did fly	flew
wind that moved	blew	row of seats	pew
did grow	grew	to carve or cut	hew
did throw	threw	prepare tea	brew
did know	knew	not old	new

1. The boys sat quietly in the first pew of their new church.

2. They had seen the crew of men working hard to build it.

3. They knew they should be quiet and listen each time they come to worship the Lord.

4. If the wind blew, it would strew papers around.

5. The bird flew down to drink some dew on the grass.

✔ Add **-es** to make the following words *plural*. NOTE: These words end with **sh, ch, s, x**, or **z**.

dishes   crosses   patches   boxes

176   Adventures in Phonics

Review Lesson of ✏ âr Words

Words that have the letters **air** make the sound of **âr** as in **stair**.

✔ Print the correct **air** words under their pictures. Use the underlined words in the sentences below.

hair	airmail	chair	repair	airfield
pair	stairway	dairy	fair	airliner

airliner   pair   hair   stairway

1. Jane saw the crew quickly repair the tire on the airplane.

2. We sent letters airmail to children in Russia.

3. Our class enjoyed the field trip to the dairy farm.

REMEMBER: When a *short vowel* word ends in a *single* consonant, that consonant is usually *doubled* before adding a suffix that begins with a vowel as in **cut ➜ cutting** and **hop ➜ hopping**.

✔ Underline the *root* words as they were before -ing was added. Divide the words into syllables. Be careful! If the *root* words end with **ll, ss, ff**, or **zz**, do not divide those double letters.

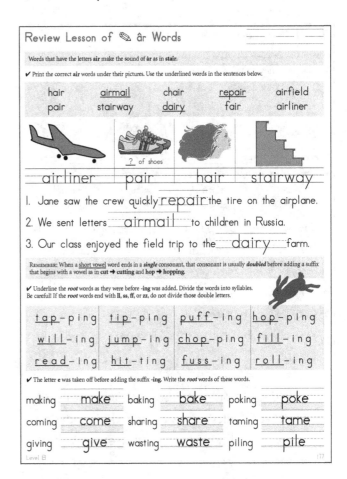

tap-ping	tip-ping	puff-ing	hop-ping
will-ing	jump-ing	chop-ping	fill-ing
read-ing	hit-ting	fuss-ing	roll-ing

✔ The letter e was taken off before adding the suffix -ing. Write the *root* words of these words.

making	make	baking	bake	poking	poke
coming	come	sharing	share	taming	tame
giving	give	wasting	waste	piling	pile

Level B   177

Page 178

Purpose

1. To review words with the soft sound **c**.

2. To have additional practice in adding suffixes **-er** and **-est** to words.

Lesson

Listen to your student read the words on Chart 37 (page 227 in the workbook).

Review the rule about doubling the single consonant in a short vowel word before adding a suffix that begins with a vowel.

      sad   sad-der   sad-dest

When your student understands the page and has given the answers orally, have him do the work independently.

Page 179

Purpose

1. To review words with the soft sound **c**.

2. To have additional practice in dividing words into syllables.

Lesson

Listen to your student read the words on Chart 37.

Talk about how a word with a prefix should be divided.

    fore–noon   dis–miss   re–plant

When your student understands the page and has given the answers orally, have him do the work independently.

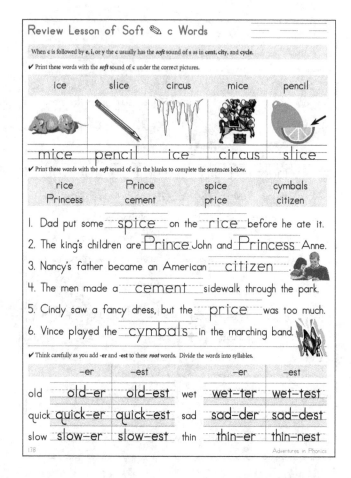

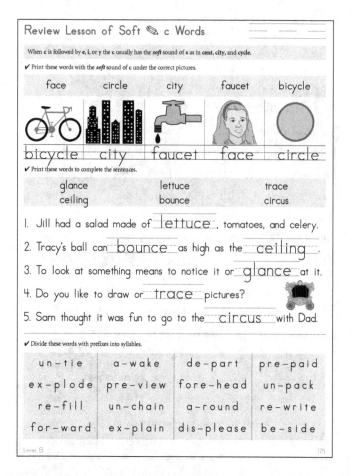

Page 180

Purpose

To learn about **Rule Five** for dividing words into syllables.

Lesson

Discuss **Rule Five**:

> When two or more consonants come between two vowels, the word is usually divided between the first two consonants.

This is an easy rule to learn.

> yel-low   fin-ger   par-rot   tur-key

When your student understands the page and has given the answers orally, have him do the work independently.

Page 181

Purpose

To review the **Five Rules** about dividing words into syllables.

Lesson

Carefully discuss each rule with your student.

When he understands the page and has given the answers orally, have him do the work by himself.

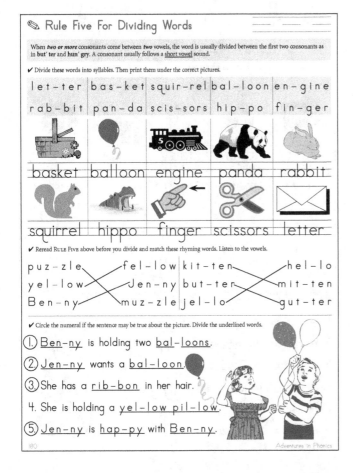

Page 182

Purpose

1. To learn about **Rule Six** for dividing words into syllables.

2. To review the rule about dividing words ending with **le** or **ckle**.

Lesson

Discuss **Rule Six**:

> When a single consonant comes between two vowels, the word is usually divided *after the consonant* if the **first** vowel sound is **short**.

> shad–ow   heav–en   sev–en

As is true about many rules, we need to listen to the vowel sound. This rule may remind us of short vowel words that end with a consonant.

> cab–in   chap–el   fig–ure

Review the rule about dividing words ending with **le** or **ckle**.

> cir–cle   rum–ble   bot–tle

> pick–le   tack–le   buck–le

When your student understands the page and has given the answers orally, have him do the work independently.

Rule Six For Dividing Words

RULE SIX: When a *single* consonant comes between *two* vowels, the word is usually divided after the consonant if the first vowel sound is *short* as in cab' in, heav' en, and shad' ow.

✔ Divide these words into syllables and print the words under the pictures. If the vowel has a *short* sound, a consonant stays with it.

cam–el	cab–in	wag–on	sev–en	rob–in
robin	wagon	camel	seven	cabin

✔ Divide these words into syllables. Listen for a short vowel. Do not divide consonant digraphs **th**.

liz–ard	rad–ish	trav–el	ped–al
heav–y	met–al	heav–en	vis–it
mel–on	fin–ish	lev–el	mod–el

Do you remember learning about words ending with **le**? You have already learned how to divide them. RULE 10 a: When a word ends in **le**, the consonant just before the **le** is usually part of the last syllable as in bu' **gle** and cat' **tle**. Divide these words into syllables and print them under the correct pictures.

ap–ple	tum–ble	tur–tle	bot–tle	peo–ple
turtle	people	bottle	apple	tumble

RULE 10 b: Words ending with **ckle** are divided after the **ck**, making **le** the last syllable as in pick' le. Divide these words into syllables as you print them on the lines provided.

tickle	tick–le	trickle	trick–le	speckle	speck–le
buckle	buck–le	freckle	freck–le	crackle	crack–le

182   Adventures in Phonics

Page 183

Purpose

1. To learn about **Rule Seven** for dividing words into syllables.

2. To review the suffix **-er**.

Lesson

Discuss **Rule Seven**:

> When a single consonant comes between two vowels, the word is usually divided *before the consonant* if the **first** vowel sound is **long**.

> pa–per   se–cret   mu–sic

Again it is important to listen to vowel sounds! This rule reminds us of words that end with a long vowel sound.

> no–tice   go–pher   so–lo
> free–dom   He–brew   lo–cal

Talk about how the suffix -er changes or modifies a word such as in:

> speak ⇒ **speak**' er

> point ⇒ **point**' er

When your student understands the page and has given the answers orally, have him do the work independently.

Rule Seven For Dividing Words

When a *single* consonant comes between *two* vowels, the word is usually divided before the consonant if the first vowel sound is *long* as in mu' sic, ze' bra, co' zy, and tu' lip.

✔ Divide these words into syllables. Divide right after the vowels that make the long vowel sound.

dai–sy	la–dy	pa–per	stu–dent	ti–ger
tiger	student	daisy	paper	lady

✔ Divide these words into syllables. Listen for a long vowel.

la–zy	le–gal	Da–vid	po–lice	lo–cate
co–zy	o–dor	mo–ment	cli–mate	ze–bra
la–bel	pro–tect	pu–pil	spi–der	mu–sic
ba–sin	la–dy	ri–der	ca–ble	tu–lip
si–lent	na–ture	pi–lot	se–cret	ho–tel

✔ Do you remember that the suffix **-er** modifies or changes a word? The **-er** has the *schwa* plus r sound. Take off the s or es from the underlined word and add the suffix **-er** as you print what each person does.

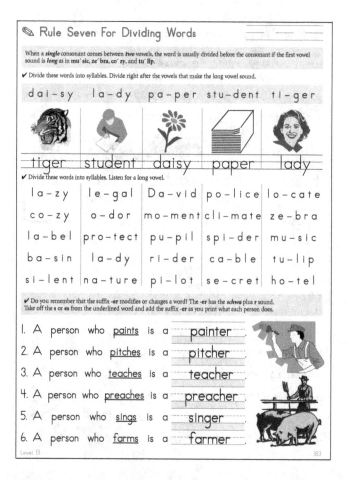

1. A person who <u>paints</u> is a   painter
2. A person who <u>pitches</u> is a   pitcher
3. A person who <u>teaches</u> is a   teacher
4. A person who <u>preaches</u> is a   preacher
5. A person who <u>sings</u> is a   singer
6. A person who <u>farms</u> is a   farmer

Level B   183

Page 184

Purpose

1. To learn that the letters **ei** usually make the long **a** sound.

2. To learn the rule about adding the suffix **-er** to words ending with a **y**.

Lesson

Teach your student that the letters **eigh** make the long vowel **a** sound. The letters **ey** may also make the long vowel **a** sound. Have him read all of the words on Chart 40 (page 228 in the workbook) until he can say them quickly.

Discuss this rule:

> When a word ends with a consonant and **y**, change the **y** to **i** when you need to add the suffixes **-er** or **-est**.

> happy   happier   happiest

When your student understands the page and has given the answers orally, have him do the work independently.

Page 185

Purpose

1. To review words with the consonant digraphs **kn** and **wr**.

2. To review words with the vowels **ei** having the long **a** vowel sound.

3. To review words with the **ear** sounds.

Lesson

Listen to your student read the words in Chart 42 (page 228 in the workbook), as well as the words on Chart 40.

When your student understands the page and has given the answers orally, have him do the work independently.

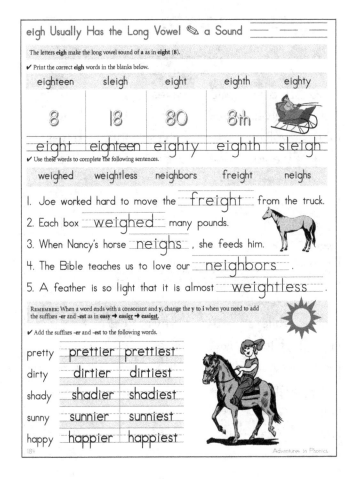

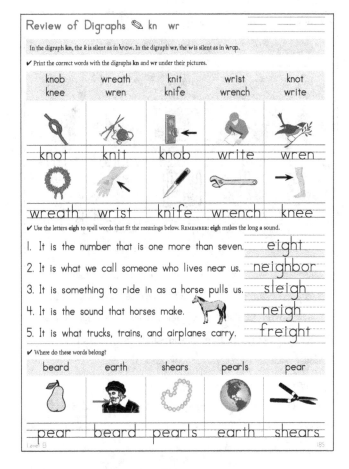

Page 186

Purpose

To work with words having the soft sound of **g**.

Lesson

Listen to your student read the words on Chart 38 (page 227 in the workbook).

Give special attention to the vowel sounds in these words with **dge** and **ge** or **nge**.

Usually the vowel is *short* before the letters **dge**.

bridge   badge   pledge

Usually the vowel is *long* before the letters **ge** or **nge**.

cage   stage   manger

When your student has carefully gone over the page with you and has given the answers orally, have him do the work independently.

Page 187

Purpose

1. To teach how to change words ending with **f** or **fe** to be *plural*.

2. To review the rules for making other words plural.

Lesson

Discuss this rule about how to change words ending with **f** or **fe** to be *plural*:

> When a word ends with **f** or **fe**, change the **f** or **fe** to **v** and add the suffix **-es** to make the word plural.

Show these examples:

wolf ⇒ wolves   life ⇒ lives

loaf ⇒ loaves   knife ⇒ knives

Carefully review the rules in the center of the lesson.

When your student has carefully gone over the page with you and has given the answers orally, have him do the work independently.

Page 188

Purpose

1. To teach one of the purposes for an **apostrophe**.

2. To review the rule for changing words ending with **f** or **fe** to be plural.

Lesson

Using the rule at the top of the lesson, explain how the apostrophe helps to show ownership. Perhaps use your student's name for an example.

book of Kelsey	⇒	Kelsey's book
paw of dog	⇒	dog's paw
dress of sister	⇒	sister's dress

When you have carefully gone over the page with your student and he has given the answers orally, have him do the work independently.

Page 189

Purpose

1. To review **Rules Six** and **Seven** about dividing words into syllables.

2. To review the use of the apostrophe to show ownership.

Lesson

Remind the student to listen to the first vowel sound in the word. This will help him to divide correctly.

Using the rules as they are written at the top of the lesson, go over the words in the exercises below for examples.

When you have carefully gone over the page with your student and he has given the answers orally, have him do the work independently.

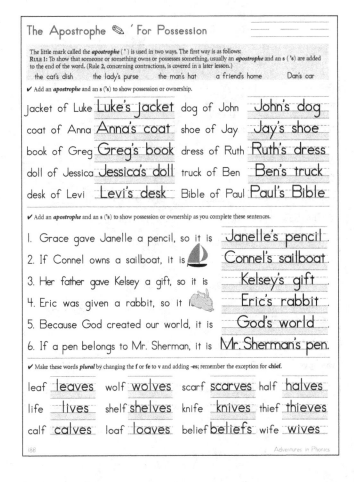

The Apostrophe ✎ ´ For Possession

The little mark called the **apostrophe** (') is used in two ways. The first way is as follows:
RULE 1: To show that someone or something owns or possesses something, usually an **apostrophe** and an s ('s) are added to the end of the word. (Rule 2, concerning contractions, is covered in a later lesson.)

the cat's dish   the lady's purse   the man's hat   a friend's home   Dan's car

✔ Add an **apostrophe** and an s ('s) to show possession or ownership.

jacket of Luke	Luke's jacket	dog of John	John's dog
coat of Anna	Anna's coat	shoe of Jay	Jay's shoe
book of Greg	Greg's book	dress of Ruth	Ruth's dress
doll of Jessica	Jessica's doll	truck of Ben	Ben's truck
desk of Levi	Levi's desk	Bible of Paul	Paul's Bible

✔ Add an **apostrophe** and an s ('s) to show possession or ownership as you complete these sentences.

1. Grace gave Janelle a pencil, so it is   Janelle's pencil
2. If Connel owns a sailboat, it is   Connel's sailboat
3. Her father gave Kelsey a gift, so it is   Kelsey's gift
4. Eric was given a rabbit, so it   Eric's rabbit
5. Because God created our world, it is   God's world
6. If a pen belongs to Mr. Sherman, it is   Mr. Sherman's pen.

✔ Make these words **plural** by changing the f or fe to v and adding -es; remember the exception for **chief**.

leaf	leaves	wolf	wolves	scarf	scarves	half	halves
life	lives	shelf	shelves	knife	knives	thief	thieves
calf	calves	loaf	loaves	belief	beliefs	wife	wives

188   Adventures in Phonics

Syllables ✎ Rules Six and Seven

RULE SIX: When a **single** consonant comes between **two** vowels, the word is usually divided after the consonant if the first vowel sound is **short** as in cab´ in, heav´ en, and moth´ er.
The short vowel needs a consonant.

RULE SEVEN: When a **single** consonant comes between **two** vowels, the word is usually divided before the consonant if the first vowel sound is **long** as in mu´ sic, ze´ bra, and co´ zy.
The long vowel can stand alone.

✔ Divide these words according to the RULES above.

finish	fin–ish	heavy	heav–y		
robin	rob–in	cover	cov–er	tiger	ti–ger
radish	rad–ish	metal	met–al	tulip	tu–lip
chapel	chap–el	legal	le–gal	pony	po–ny
wagon	wag–on	story	stor–y	label	la–bel
river	riv–er	paper	pa–per	cozy	co–zy
lady	la–dy	lazy	la–zy	motor	mo–tor
travel	trav–el	regal	re–gal	panda	pan–da
cabin	cab–in	seven	sev–en	zebra	ze–bra

✔ Do you remember how to use an **apostrophe** and s? The **cap** that belongs to **Sam** is written: **Sam's cap**.

1. When William eats an apple, it is   William's apple
2. If a kangaroo has food, it is the   kangaroo's food
3. If a squirrel found a nut, it is the   squirrel's nut
4. Tom got a letter in the mail, so it is   Tom's letter

Level B   189

Page 190

Purpose

To teach the second purpose for an **apostrophe**.

Lesson

Using the rule at the top of the lesson, explain how the apostrophe helps make two special words into one word. Go over this lesson carefully for good understanding.

When you have carefully gone over the page with your student and he has given the answers orally, he may then print the answers independently.

Page 191

Purpose

1. To teach that the letter **s** may sometimes have the sound of **z**.
2. To apply both rules of the **apostrophe**.

Lesson

Listen closely as your student says the words in the first exercise to you. There may be a few words that could have either the **s** or **z** sound.

Review each apostrophe rule, as well as the exercises below them.

When you have carefully gone over the page with your student and he has given the answers orally, he may then print the answers independently.

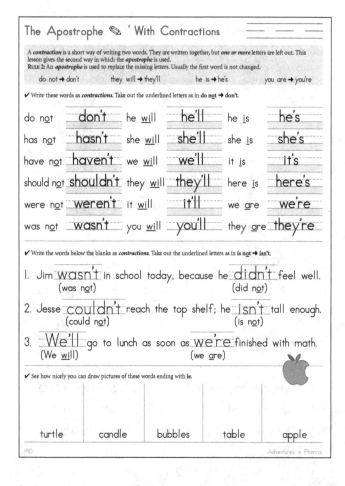

The Apostrophe ✎ ' With Contractions

A **contraction** is a short way of writing two words. They are written together, but *one or more* letters are left out. This lesson gives the second way in which the *apostrophe* is used.
RULE 2: An *apostrophe* is used to replace the missing letters. Usually the first word is not changed.

do not → don't   they will → they'll   he is → he's   you are → you're

✔ Write these words as *contractions*. Take out the underlined letters as in **do not → don't**.

do not	**don't**	he will	**he'll**	he is	**he's**
has not	**hasn't**	she will	**she'll**	she is	**she's**
have not	**haven't**	we will	**we'll**	it is	**it's**
should not	**shouldn't**	they will	**they'll**	here is	**here's**
were not	**weren't**	it will	**it'll**	we are	**we're**
was not	**wasn't**	you will	**you'll**	they are	**they're**

✔ Write the words below the blanks as *contractions*. Take out the underlined letters as in **is not → isn't**.

1. Jim **wasn't** in school today, because he **didn't** feel well.
   (was not)   (did not)

2. Jesse **couldn't** reach the top shelf; he **isn't** tall enough.
   (could not)   (is not)

3. **We'll** go to lunch as soon as **we're** finished with math.
   (We will)   (we are)

✔ See how nicely you can draw pictures of these words ending with **le**.

| turtle | candle | bubbles | table | apple |

190   Adventures in Phonics

The Sound of z Made by ✎ s

Sometimes an s can sound like a **z** as in **rose** and **teams**.

✔ Print s or z on the lines to show the sound made by the s.

mouse	**s**	peels	**z**	gates	**s**	needless	**s**
obeys	**z**	six	**s**	has	**z**	wheels	**z**
horse	**s**	arise	**z**	nose	**z**	rains	**z**

Apostrophe RULE 1: To show that someone or something owns or possesses something, usually an *apostrophe* and an s ('s) are added to the end of the word as in **Charles Spurgeon's son**.

✔ Add 's to the underlined words to show ownership, and print the phrases to complete the sentences.

1. The white hat on Naomi is   **Naomi's hat**
2. The bow on the bear is the   **bear's bow**
3. The dress on the bunny is the   **bunny's dress**
4. The sail on the boat is the   **boat's sail**
5. The shirt belongs to Jay; it is   **Jay's shirt**

Apostrophe Rule 2: An *apostrophe* is put in the place of the missing letters that are removed when forming a *contraction*. Usually the first word is not changed.
Contractions can also be written with the word **have** as in **we have → we've**.

✔ Print these words as *contractions* by taking out the underlined letters and adding an *apostrophe*.

we have	**we've**	has not	**hasn't**	you have	**you've**
would not	**wouldn't**	they have	**they've**	let us	**let's**
we are	**we're**	she is	**she's**	he is	**he's**
they are	**they're**	should not	**shouldn't**	could not	**couldn't**

Level B   191

Page 192

Purpose

1. To teach additional ways to change some words to be plural.

2. To review rules for making words *plural*.

Lesson

Have your student read these words with you, explaining that these words need to be changed in this way to become plural.

man	men	goose	geese
woman	women	foot	feet
mouse	mice	tooth	teeth

Carefully review the rules for making words to be plural. After you have listened to your student answer the lesson, ask him to print the lesson independently.

Page 193

Purpose

To give additional practice in changing words to be plural.

Lesson

Carefully review the rules for making words plural, using the words in the list to apply the rules.

After you have gone over the entire lesson and have heard your student give the answers orally, have him complete the page independently.

✎ More Plural Forms of Words

Some words form their *plurals* in an unusual way as in **ox ➤ oxen** and **mouse ➤ mice**.

✔ Print these *plural* words where they belong. Use these words to complete the sentences below.

| feet | children | women | teeth | men | geese |

tooth __teeth__   foot __feet__   woman __women__
child __children__   man __men__   goose __geese__

1. As the __children__ smiled, their missing __teeth__ showed.

2. The __women__ screamed when they saw the two mice.

3. The __men__ chased the two noisy __geese__ into the barn.

4. The baby's __feet__ were perfectly formed by our Creator.

REMEMBER the following RULES for making words *plural*:
1. To make many words *plural*, just add -s as in *cats*.
2. To make words *plural* that end with sh, ch, s, x, or z, add -es as in *dishes*.
3. To make words *plural* that end with y follow the next two RULES:
   a. Add -s if y comes after a vowel as in *boys*.
   b. Change the y to i, and add -es, if y comes after a consonant as in *city ➤ cities*.

✔ Think of the RULES above as you make these words plural.

peach	__peaches__	toy	__toys__	turkey	__turkeys__
frog	__frogs__	box	__boxes__	fly	__flies__
sky	__skies__	jacket	__jackets__	injury	__injuries__
girl	__girls__	tax	__taxes__	valley	__valleys__
tray	__trays__	waltz	__waltzes__	watch	__watches__
glass	__glasses__	bush	__bushes__	ash	__ashes__

192   Adventures in Phonics

✎ Review of Plural Words

When a word ends in f or fe, change the f or fe to v and add the suffix -es to make the word *plural* as in **calf ➤ calves** and **knife ➤ knives**. Two exceptions are: **belief ➤ beliefs** and **chief ➤ chiefs**.

✔ Think of the above RULE as you make these words plural.

belief	__beliefs__	scarf	__scarves__	wolf	__wolves__
calf	__calves__	half	__halves__	knife	__knives__
life	__lives__	loaf	__loaves__	leaf	__leaves__
thief	__thieves__	chief	__chiefs__	shelf	__shelves__

REMEMBER the following RULES for making words *plural*:
1. To make many words *plural*, just add -s as in *cats*.
2. To make words *plural* that end with sh, ch, s, x, or z, add -es as in *dishes*.
3. To make words *plural* that end with y follow the next two RULES:
   a. Add -s if y comes after a vowel as in *boys*.
   b. Change the y to i, and add -es, if y comes after a consonant as in *city ➤ cities*.

✔ Think of the above RULES as you make these words plural.

church	__churches__	table	__tables__	boy	__boys__
fox	__foxes__	dress	__dresses__	brush	__brushes__
turkey	__turkeys__	lunch	__lunches__	fly	__flies__
match	__matches__	box	__boxes__	city	__cities__
girl	__girls__	cherry	__cherries__	valley	__valleys__

A few words become *plural* in special ways as in **man ➤ men**.

✔ Match the following words to their unusual *plurals*.

man — women   child — mice   goose — workmen
tooth — teeth   mouse — feet   ox — geese
woman — men   foot — children   workman — oxen

Level B   193

Page 194

Purpose

To teach **Rule Eight** about dividing words into syllables.

Lesson

Discuss **Rule Eight** with your student:

> If a vowel is sounded alone in a word, it forms a syllable by itself.

This is not a difficult rule to learn, but you should give as much help as needed to teach a clear understanding of dividing the syllables.

a–long	a–way	i–dol
o–pen	o–cean	mel–o–dy

Use the list of words in the lesson for examples.

When you have carefully gone over the page with your student and he has given the answers orally, he may then print the answers independently.

Page 195

Purpose

To teach **Rule Nine** about dividing words into syllables.

Lesson

Discuss **Rule Nine** with your student:

> When two vowels come together and are sounded separately, divide the word between the two vowels.

po–em	u–su–al	cre–ate
sci–ence	li–on	ro–de–o

Use the list of words in the lesson for examples.

When you have carefully gone over the page with your student and he has given the answers orally, he may then print the answers independently.

* Note that in the second exercise on page 195, the word *guardian* may also be divided as **guard–i–an**.

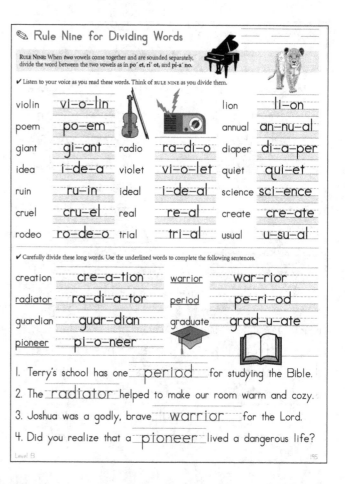

Page 196

Purpose

To review the first five rules for dividing words into syllables.

Lesson

As you discuss each rule one at a time, use the words under that rule for examples. Hopefully, your student has learned much from these lessons on dividing words. These rules will also be reviewed in other grades, which will help him to gain a better understanding of them.

When you have carefully gone over the page and he has given the answers orally, he may then print the answers independently.

Page 197

Purpose

To review the last five rules for dividing words into syllables.

Lesson

As you discuss each rule one at a time, use the words under that rule for examples. Some of the rules are easier than others, but hopefully your student has learned much from these lessons on dividing words. These rules will also be reviewed in other grades, which will help him to gain a better understanding of them.

Under **Rules Six** and **Seven**, have the student divide the words in the boxes and print the correct words under their pictures. Under **Rules Eight**, **Nine**, and **Ten**, have the student divide the words according to the respective rule being reviewed.

When you have carefully gone over the page and he has given the answers orally, he may then print the answers independently.

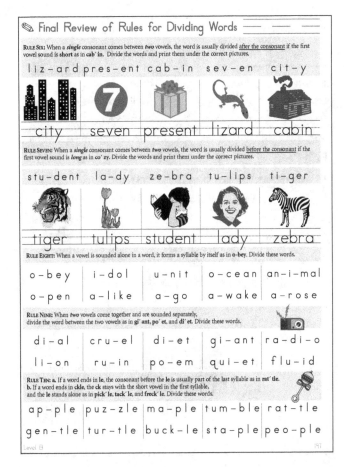

Page 198

Purpose

To teach the definition of a **synonym**.

Lesson

Discuss the definition of a *synonym*:

> A word that has the **same** or a **similar** meaning to another word.

Ask your student what words would mean the *same* as the words in **bold** below. There are several possible answers for many of the words.

happy	(glad)	**house**	(home)
close	(near)	**talk**	(speak)
woods	(forest)	**repair**	(fix)
shop	(store)	**quiet**	(still)

After you have carefully gone over the page with your student and he has given the answers orally, he may then print the answers independently.

Page 199

Purpose

To teach the definition of a **synonym**.

Lesson

Discuss the definition of a *synonym*:

> A word that has the **same** or a **similar** meaning to another word.

Ask your student what words would mean the *same* as the words in **bold** below. There are several possible answers for many of the words.

fall	(drop)	**child**	(infant)
small	(tiny)	**swift**	(fast)
level	(even)	**listen**	(hear)
store	(shop)	**funny**	(silly)

After you have carefully gone over the page with your student and he has given the answers orally, he may then print the answers independently.

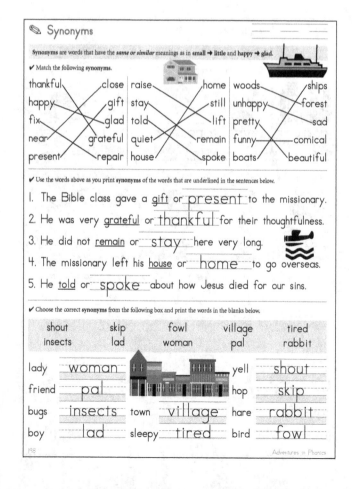

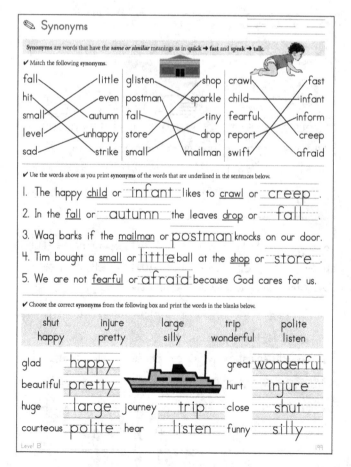

Page 200

Purpose

To teach the definition of an **antonym**.

Lesson

Discuss the definition of an **antonym**:

A word that has the **opposite** or **almost opposite** meaning of another word.

Ask your student what words would have the *opposite* meaning of the words in **bold** below. There are several possible answers for many of the words.

strong	(weak)	**wet**	(dry)
happy	(sad)	**light**	(dark)
near	(far)	**thick**	(thin)
many	(few)	**spend**	(save)

After you have carefully gone over the page with your student and he has given the answers orally, he may then print the answers independently.

Page 201

Purpose

To teach the definition of an **antonym**.

Lesson

Discuss the definition of an **antonym**:

A word that has the **opposite** or **almost opposite** meaning of another word.

Ask your student what words would have the *opposite* meaning of the words in **bold** below. There are several possible answers for many of the words.

under	(over)	**asleep**	(awake)
fast	(slow)	**go**	(come)
hot	(cold)	**hard**	(soft)
young	(old)	**lose**	(win)

After you have carefully gone over the page with your student and he has given the answers orally, he may then print the answers independently.

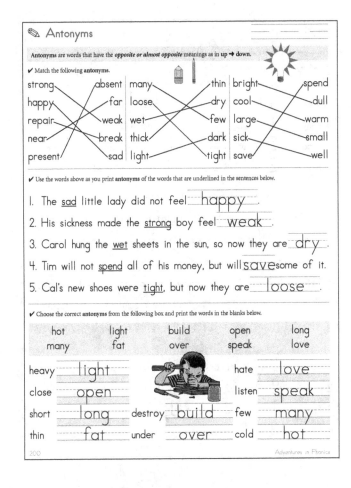

Page 202

Purpose

To review the definitions of **synonyms** and **antonyms**.

Lesson

Discuss both of the definitions. Go slowly through the lesson, giving sufficient time for the student to think about the words he is comparing.

After you have carefully gone over the page with your student and he has given the answers orally, he may then complete the answers independently.

Page 203

Purpose

To teach the definition of a **homonym**.

Lesson

Discuss the definition of *homonyms*:

> Words that **sound alike**, but have different meanings and spellings.

Ask your student to fill in the correct homonyms in the following sets of sentences.

My *blue* dress has lace around the collar.

The strong wind _____ the shed over.

The basketball went *through* the hoop.

Bill _____ the baseball across home plate.

Talk about the meaning of these homonyms.

peek	peak	break	brake
road	rode	weigh	way

After you have carefully discussed the page with your student and he has given the answers orally, he may then complete the answers independently.

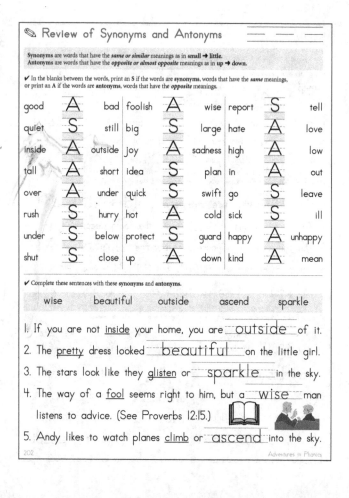

Page 204

Purpose

1. To teach the three possible sounds of the digraph **ch**.

2. To give additional practice in adding the suffix **-ed** and saying the sound it makes as it is added to a short vowel sound word.

Lesson

Discuss the three sounds of **ch** as they are mentioned in the directions. Many of the **ch** words may be new to your student. Go slowly through the lesson as he gives you the answers. If the student has questions about the sound of the suffix **-ed**, refer to page 140 in the workbook or page 71 in this teacher's guide.

When you feel your student is ready, ask him to complete the written work independently.

Page 205

Purpose

To teach the sounds of the digraphs **gh** and **ph**.

Lesson

Introduce these sounds and listen to your student read the words in Chart 43 (page 228 in the workbook). You may also use the **ph** flashcard.

Many of the words in this lesson will be new to your student. Go slowly through the lists and exercises as he tells you the answers.

When you feel your student is ready, ask him to complete the written work independently.

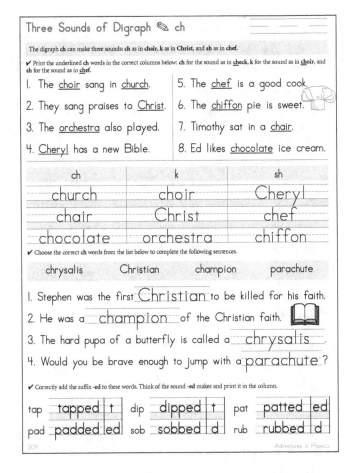

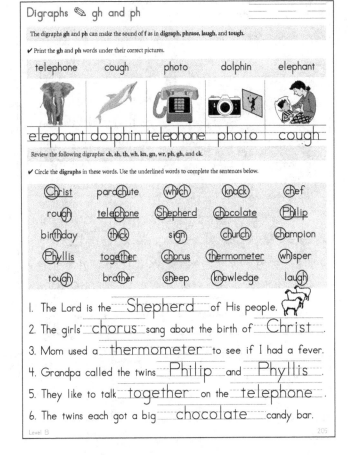

Page 206

Purpose

To teach about the suffix -tion.

Lesson

The suffix **-tion** modifies or changes a root word to help it have a special meaning or use. The **-tion** makes the sound of *shun*.

Read and discuss these words with your student.

create	creation
invent	invention
elect	election
inject	injection
introduce	introduction
celebrate	celebration
educate	education

Many of the words in this lesson will be new to him. Go slowly through the lists and exercises as he tells you the answers.

When you feel your student is ready, ask him to complete the written work independently.

Page 207

Purpose

To teach about the suffix -sion.

Lesson

The suffix **-sion** modifies or changes a root word to help it have a special meaning or use. The **-sion** makes the sound of *shun* or *zhun*.

Read and discuss these words with your student.

collide	collision
discuss	discussion
divide	division
admit	admission
exclude	exclusion
revise	revision
conclude	conclusion

Many of the words in this lesson will be new to him. Go slowly through the lists and exercises as he tells you the answers.

When you feel your student is ready, ask him to complete the written work independently.

Words Ending with ✏ –tion

The letters **-tion** make the sound of *shun* as in **nation** and **vacation**.

✔ Add **-tion** to these words and read them. Use the underlined words to complete the sentences below.

afflic**tion**	elec**tion**	na**tion**	resurrec**tion**
frac**tion**	rela**tion**	mo**tion**	informa**tion**
inven**tion**	crea**tion**	auc**tion**	introduc**tion**
educa**tion**	vaca**tion**	cau**tion**	celebra**tion**
forma**tion**	injec**tion**	sta**tion**	circula**tion**

1. We praise the Lord for His wonderful **creation**.
2. The book had **information** on the **invention** of radios.
3. We are praying for Al, who has a serious **affliction**.
4. In the spring we have a week's **vacation** as we have a **celebration** of Jesus Christ's **resurrection**.

A syllable is made up of *one or more* letters pronounced together as a *single* sound with a vowel. Each **syllable** has a vowel sound as in **strong′**, **neigh′ bor**, **in-ven′ tion**, **stee′ ple**, and **tel′ e-phone**.

✔ Write the number of syllables that are in these words. Listen and think as you say each word.

trust	1	invitation	4	forgiving	3	thoughtful	2
scrubbing	2	slept	1	buckle	2	truthful	2
spring	1	kind	1	battle	2	education	4
telephone	3	knocked	1	careful	2	vacation	3

Words Ending with ✏ –sion

The letters **-sion** make the sound of *shun* or *zhun* as in **discussion** and **division**.

✔ Add **-sion** to these words and read them. Use the underlined words to complete the sentences below.

colli**sion**	admis**sion**	conclu**sion**	televi**sion**
discus**sion**	exclu**sion**	inva**sion**	confu**sion**
divi**sion**	revi**sion**	excur**sion**	fu**sion**

1. You have had many hours of talking or **discussion**.
2. It is better to read a book than to watch **television**.
3. Terry was glad that the story had a happy **conclusion**.
4. There was **confusion** as the children looked for their shoes.
5. We prayed for a friend who was in a car **collision**.

Do you remember that sometimes digraphs **gh** and **ph** make the sound of **f** as in **laugh** and **telephone**? Do you also remember that the digraph **ch** makes three different sounds as in **chip**, **chef**, and **choir**?

✔ Use the words in the list below to complete the following sentences.

elephant	chauffeur	phonics	spinach	rough

1. A **chauffeur** came to take the bride to church.
2. God made something like a finger at the end of the trunk of an **elephant**. Would it like to eat **spinach**?
3. Philip enjoyed reading because he learned **phonics**.
4. The hardworking farmer had very strong, **rough** hands.

Page 208

Purpose

To review words having different sounds of the vowel **o**.

Lesson

As the directions say, this lesson includes three of the sounds of the vowel **o**. Read the lines of words several times to help your student to know the sounds well.

ô	ŏ	ō
soft	shop	home
dog	rock	comb
frog	pond	low
cloth	drop	goat
off	sob	own

Review the rule about changing the **y** to **i** before adding **-ed** to words ending with a **y** next to a consonant. Do not change the **y** when it is next to a vowel.

After you have gone over the entire lesson with your student and you feel he is ready, ask him to complete the written work independently.

Page 209

Purpose

To review the two rules for using the **apostrophe**.

Lesson

Follow the directions as they discuss the rules one at a time. Use the examples in the lesson as you review.

After you have gone over the entire lesson with your student and you feel he is ready, ask him to complete the written work independently.

Hopefully, you both can see an improvement in his printing.

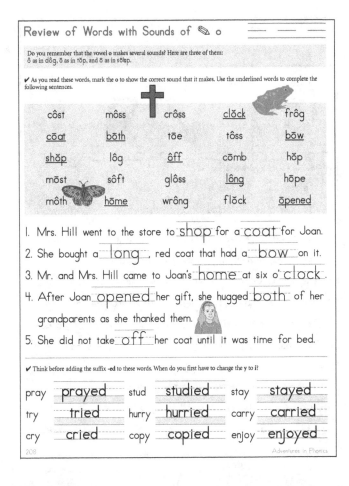

Page 210

Purpose

To review the definitions of **synonyms**, **antonyms**, and homonyms.

Lesson

Carefully discuss the definitions of these three big words with easy meanings.

After you have slowly gone over the entire lesson with your student and you feel he is ready, ask him to complete the written work independently.

Page 211

Purpose

To review words with the short vowel sound of **u** that is made by **o** and **a**.

Lesson

After you have gone over this lesson with your student and you feel he is ready, ask him to complete the written work independently.

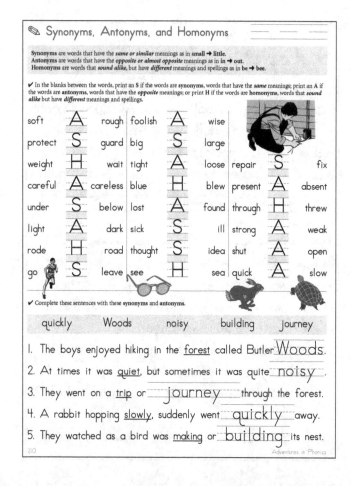

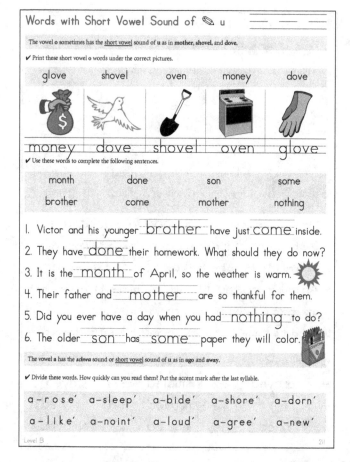

Page 212

Purpose

1. To introduce the student to *alphabetizing* words from a list.

2. To use a **dictionary** to find the meaning of words the student does not know.

Lesson

After you have gone over this lesson with your student and you feel he is ready, ask him to complete the written work independently.

Page 213

Purpose

1. To introduce the student to *alphabetizing* words from a list.

2. To use a **dictionary** to find the meaning of words the student does not know.

Lesson

Explain that the three words *hands,* *head,* and *heart* in the exercise at the bottom of the page are placed according to the second or fourth letters in the words.

After you have gone over this lesson with your student and you feel he is ready, ask him to complete the written work independently.

Congratulations! You finished this book!

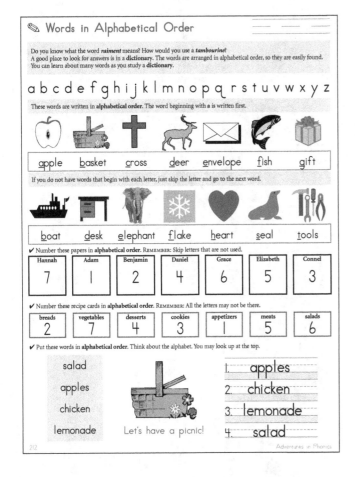

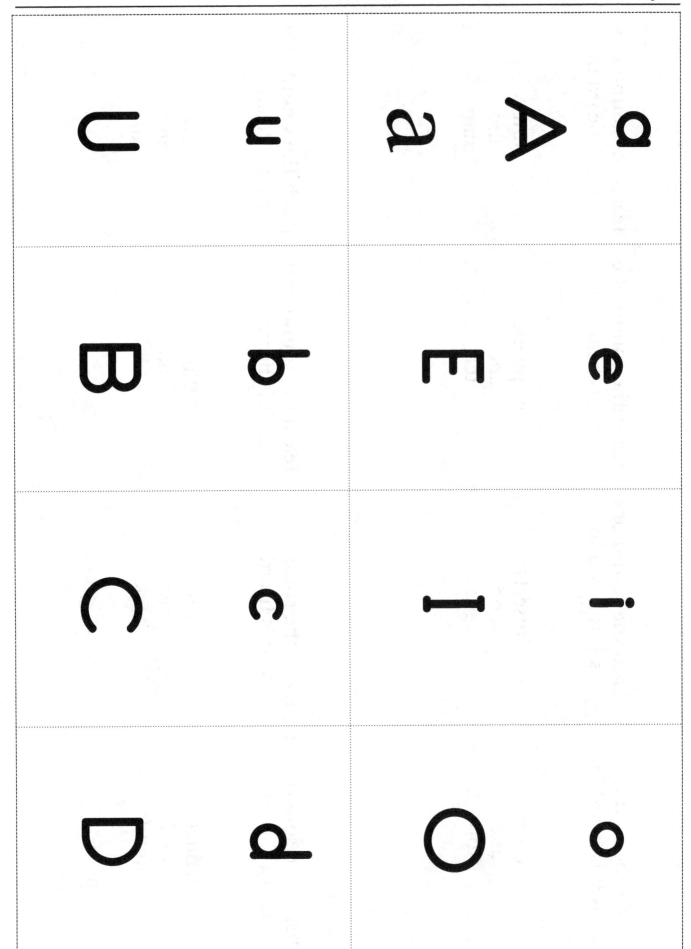

Teach the **sound** of **a**
as it is heard in

ant
and
man

Teach the **sound** of **u**
as it is heard in

up
and
mud

Teach the **sound** of **e**
as it is heard in

elephant
and
ten

Teach the **sound** of **b**
as it is heard in

Bible
and
cub

Teach the **sound** of **i**
as it is heard in

insects
and
six

Teach the **sound** of **c**
as it is heard in

cat
and
back

Teach the **sound** of **o**
as it is heard in

otter
and
top

Teach the **sound** of **d**
as it is heard in

duck
and
mud

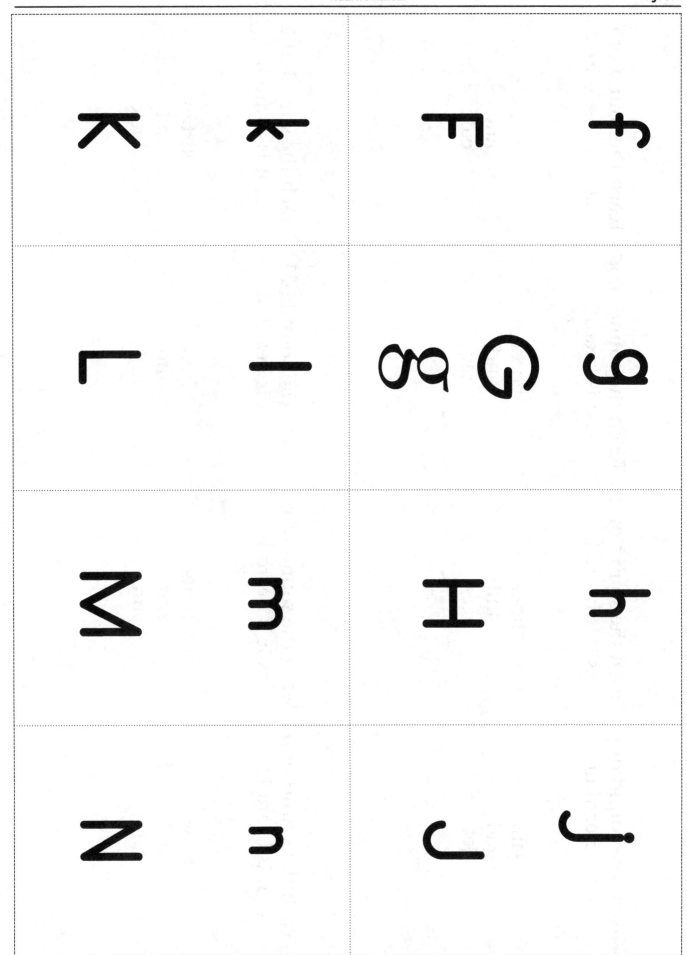

Teach the **sound** of **f**
as it is heard in

fox
and
cuff

Teach the **sound** of **k**
as it is heard in

kitten
and
duck

Teach the **sound** of **g**
as it is heard in

goose
and
tag

Teach the **sound** of **l**
as it is heard in

lion
and
hill

Teach the **sound** of **h**
as it is heard in

horse
and
heart

Teach the **sound** of **m**
as it is heard in

mother
and
jam

Teach the **sound** of **j**
as it is heard in

jam
and
jet

Teach the **sound** of **n**
as it is heard in

nose
and
fan

Teach the **sound** of **s** as it is heard in

squirrel
and
dress

Teach the **sound** of **r** as it is heard in

rabbit
and
car

(**kw**)
Teach the **sound** of **qu** as it is heard in

quail
and
queen

Teach the **sound** of **p** as it is heard in

pear
and
top

(**ks**)
Teach the **sound** of **x** as it is heard in

ax
and
box

Teach the **sound** of **w** as it is heard in

walrus
and
world

Teach the **sound** of **v** as it is heard in

vine
and
cave

Teach the **sound** of **t** as it is heard in

turtle
and
hat

e
ee
ea
ey

Y

y

i
ie

Z

z

o
oa
o‾e
ow

sh

ew
u‾e
ui

ay
a‾e
ai

Teach the **sound** of **a**
as it is heard in

sail, ape
and
day

Teach the **sound** of **sh**
as it is heard in

ship
and
fish

Teach the **sound** of **z**
as it is heard in

zebra
and
buzz

Teach the **sound** of **y**
as it is heard in

yard
and
yawn

Teach the **sound** of **u**
as it is heard in

suit, mule
and
new

Teach the **sound** of **o**
as it is heard in

go, goat,
home, and
snow

Teach the **sound** of **i**
as it is heard in

five, pie,
and
fly

Teach the **sound** of **e**
as it is heard in

me, tree,
ear, and
key

oo(

or

oo

oy

oi

ch

er
ir
ur
(w)or
(w)ear

ou

ow

är

Teach the **sound** of **ar**
as it is heard in

arm
and
car

Teach the **sound** of **er**
as it is heard in

verse, girl,
turtle, earth,
and world

Teach the **sound** of **oi**
as it is heard in

oil
and
boy

Teach the **sound** of **or**
as it is heard in

corn
and
fork

Teach the **sound** of **ow**
as it is heard in

cow
and
mouse

Teach the **sound** of **ch**
as it is heard in

church
and
lunch

Teach the **sound** of o͞o
as it is heard in

moon
and
tool

Teach the **sound** of o͝o
as it is heard in

book
and
good

o al

aw au

ough th

augh th

wh

kn

th th

gn

ar arr

air err

ear ere

wr

ph

Teach the **sound** of **ph** as it is heard in

phone
and
photo

Teach the **sound** of **âr** as it is heard in

Mary, carrot, chair, berry, bear, and where

Teach the <u>two</u> **sounds** of **th** as these are heard in

think, bath, and the, mother

Teach the **sound** of **wh** as it is heard in

whip
and
whale

Teach that the **w** is silent when it is followed by **r** as in

write
and
wreath

Teach that the **g** is silent when it is followed by **n** as in

gnaw
and
gnat

Teach that the **k** is silent when it is followed by **n** as in

knit
and
know

Teach the **sound** of **ô** as it is heard in

dog, talk, saw, haul, **bought,** and **daughter**